Grief Nuggets

Grief Nuggets

Daily Insights For The Grieving Heart

RICK BERGH

Grief Nuggets
Daily Insights For The Grieving Heart

Copyright © 2024 by Rick Bergh

All rights reserved. No part of this publication may be reproduced, stored in or introduced into a retrieval system, or transmitted, in any form, or by any means (electronic, mechanical, photocopying, recording or otherwise), without the prior permission of the publisher.

This publication is not intended as a substitute for the advice of health care professionals.

ISBNs:
978-1-988082-14-1 (paperback)
978-1-988082-33-2 (hardback)

Published by:
Beacon Mount Publishing
26 Bow Meadows Drive
Cochrane, Alberta, T4C 1M1
Canada
www.rickbergh.com

Printed and bound in the United States of America.

*This book is dedicated to Kevin Lewis and
all my friends at First Memorial in
Victoria, British Columbia.
Thank you for believing in grief education and
supporting me in my journey
as grief educator and counsellor.*

ACKNOWLEDGEMENTS

This book has taken four years to write. Every week, I would sit down to find one ordinary, commonplace word to encapsulate a lesson or a thought that might be helpful for a grieving heart.

Recognizing that most people who are grieving don't want to digest a lot of information, I settled on the concept of the *grief nugget*. People's encouraging feedback led me to compile 365 of these small nuggets to be used daily by grievers.

I want to thank my wife, Erica, for her massive contributions to this book. As my frontline editor, she has added her creative touch and offered insightful feedback. I could not have written this book without her. I love you, Erica.

And thank you to God for EVERYTHING! I am blessed beyond measure.

PREFACE

Coming out of thirty-five years of companioning people in almost every grief experience imaginable, I share these insights for your journey.

Will you agree with all of them? Perhaps not, but I encourage you to consider how they might be helpful to you in your particular grief narrative.

I owe much to the clients whom I counsel. They often use simple words or metaphors to express complicated thoughts, feelings or behaviours that they experience on their grief journey. This book shares many of their insights, directly or indirectly, from their lived experience.

Perhaps these *nuggets* will help you find your "grieving voice" through language that allows you to articulate your own reactions to loss, enabling you to share your experience with others.

Please don't rush through these *nuggets*. Sit with each one. Be open to how they speak to your situation. If you are comfortable doing so, take small steps to move forward.

Every twenty-one days you will be invited to reflect upon a *Curious Question*. This will give you an opportunity to journal about a given question.

So, go ahead—take your pen out and write. You may find yourself returning to your insights at a later date.

Rick Bergh

Grief Nuggets

DAY 1
MOVING

You will survive and you will find purposes in the chaos. Moving on doesn't mean letting go.
–Mary Van Haute

The first phrase I usually hear from a grieving person is this: "I wish I'd had more time with them. One more conversation. One more hug. One more special occasion celebrated. But it just didn't happen."

Time ran out.

We're reminded about the moments of our lives and how we choose to spend them.

The time that you *did* have with your loved one—what was that like? What moments did you enjoy that can never be taken away from you?

DAY 2
DAZE

*The fact that something has happened to a million
other people diminishes neither grief nor joy.*
—Unknown

Do you ever feel like you're in a daze? You don't have the concentration you wish you had? Your mind is fuzzy, unclear? You can't remember things you used to? You forget names?

Grief wreaks havoc with your cortisol levels. Your body is under duress when you grieve. Fight or flight—it's magnified. That's what stress and grief do. There is so much going on in your life at every level during loss, and your body is responding by releasing cortisol—to protect you, actually.

Managing it with healthy practices such as good sleep, healthy eating patterns and exercise is a great start and will help bring your cortisol levels back to normal.

But be patient with yourself—it may take some time to stop feeling like you're in a daze.

DAY 3
PENCIL

Distance is temporary, but our love is permanent. This may be the last time I see you, but if you keep me in your heart, together we shall be eternal; if you believe, we shall never part.
–Thomas Campbell

When I write, I usually use a pen. Occasionally, I use a pencil.

One reason I use a pencil is so that I can erase and start over again if I need to. It's so simple, so uncomplicated. I just erase—and it's gone.

That's so different from losing a loved one.

You can't erase a story that's forever written in your heart.

It's not erasable. It's stronger than permanent marker—and that's a good thing.

DAY 4
NORMAL

An abnormal reaction to an abnormal situation is normal behavior.
—Viktor E. Frankl, Man's Search for Meaning

"Is this normal?"

I have been asked this question so many times as a grief counsellor. What's normal is that we each grieve differently.

What is normal for one person may not be normal for you or anyone else. Grief can't be put in a tidy box, nor can it be compared with another's grief journey.

What *is* normal is what's happening in you as a result of missing someone special.

Normal is personal.

DAY 5
IDENTITY

Grit your teeth and let it hurt. Don't deny it, don't be overwhelmed by it. It will not last forever.
—Rabbi Harold Kushner

"Who am I now?"

This is a question I hear often—especially when someone experiences the loss of a significant person in their life.

You may be asking yourself, "Who am I now without this person?" You were in a relationship and now this person is gone, causing a cataclysmic shift in your identity. You were a spouse, a partner. You were a parent. You were a caregiver. But who are you or what are you now?

Every person contributes to the make-up of who we are. They've impacted us in some way. In many cases, they've played a huge role in our lives and vice versa.

So how do you live in the vacuum of their absence?

There's a little of them in you. Or maybe there's even a lot of them in you. You can carry them forward by being who you are—they were and are still a big part of your identity.

DAY 6
TWO

*Everything that we see is a shadow cast
by that which we do not see.*
–MARTIN LUTHER KING, JR.

1) Grief is the reaction to what you miss, that you *no longer* have, that used to be.

2) Grief is the reaction to what you miss, that you *never* had but always hoped for.

I WONDER WHICH OF these definitions you feel most applies to you? Or perhaps both do.

Write down what you miss most. Consider these things as gifts that were given to you because you were in relationship with this person.

Both definitions are important in your grief journey—what you miss and what you didn't have.

DAY 7
STRONG

For everything, there is a season, and a time for every purpose under heaven: a time to be born, and a time to die; a time to break down, and a time to build up, a time to cast away stones, and a time to gather stones together; a time to keep silence, and a time to speak.
—King Solomon

WHY DO YOU have to be strong? You had someone die who was important to you and whom you loved.

Strong for others? Is that the reason? Your heart is broken and deserves some time to hurt.

You don't have to be the strong one.

DAY 8
FOG

I don't know why they call it heartbreak. It feels like every part of my body is broken too.
—Chloe Woodward

Brain fog is a real thing. Don't be surprised if your mind is not as clear as it was prior to your loss.

Do you feel like you're drifting or that you don't have full control of your body, mind or emotions?

Grief triggers various types of stress hormones and your cortisol levels are out of whack when you grieve.

Do you wonder when things will go back to the way they were?

Life can't be the same as it was before—your loved one isn't physically present.

You will likely feel that you are in this fog for a while yet. But give it some time—the fog *will* lift.

DAY 9
CLOSURE

Death ends a life, not a relationship.
—Jack Lemmon

Have you been told that you need to find *closure* in your grief journey?

Here's one definition of *closure* according to the dictionary. *Closure* is...

- a satisfying sense of finality
- an attempt to "move on" following the **termination** of a relationship
- something that you once counted on as very important to your life is over and done

Finality. Letting go of what once was. Termination. Is that what you want your grief experience to be? I'd be surprised if you said *yes* to that.

You may want to find a new way to talk about your grief that doesn't include the word *closure*.

DAY 10
KLEENEX

Tears are the silent language of grief.
–Voltaire

Tears are a gift. So is Kleenex. You've probably gone through your fair share recently.

Your tears have flowed whether by yourself or in the presence of others. It's a good thing. We were created to feel deeply about those whom we love.

Did you know that emotional tears—the ones associated with grief and sadness—contain a natural painkiller that neither basal nor reflex tears have?

So, don't hold back. Let your tears flow. You can always buy more Kleenex.

DAY 11
VOICE

What we once enjoyed and deeply loved we can never lose, for all that we love deeply becomes part of us.
–Helen Keller

Have you ever said, "I wish I could hear my loved one's voice just one more time?"

When you're used to hearing your loved one's voice and now there is only silence, it's really tough. You keep wanting to hear them call out your name. You answer the phone and hope you'll hear their voice on the other end.

These are normal sentiments.

Perhaps you can hear their voice in your head. OK, it's not the same, but because you had a relationship with your loved one, you can still have a conversation with them—their voice is indelibly imbedded in your mind.

What would that voice say to you, do you think?

DAY 12
DESCRIBE

Death ends a life, not a relationship. All the love you created is still there. All the memories are still there. You live on in the hearts of everyone you have touched and nurtured while you were here.
—Mitch Albom

If you were to describe your loved one in just a few words, what would they be?

Every single person is special and has a unique personality.

When we take time to describe a person, we realize what it was we liked about them and how they contributed something to our life.

So, go ahead, put into words what this person was like and what you loved about them.

DAY 13
EYES

*'Tis better to have loved and lost than
never to have loved at all.*
—Alfred Lord Tennyson

We humans are incredibly made. We have the capacity to "see" past experiences, even when they aren't currently taking place. This is called visual memory or what is sometimes called your "mind's eye." Our visual memory takes a snapshot of an event and stores it long-term in the hippocampus. Most of our memories are in the unconscious part of our mind, but those memories that are connected to strong emotions are the easiest to remember.

So, when we *see* something that is linked to an experience that we had with our loved one, it may well trigger a memory.

Don't be surprised when this happens to you. It's bringing back an emotional memory connected with that person—shared events that were important to you.

DAY 14
TITLE

The best and most beautiful things in the world cannot be seen or even touched. They must be felt with the heart.
–Helen Keller

To be in relationship with a human being is a gift. Honoring your grief because it is tied to a loving relationship is an important part of your grief journey. As you shared life together, you have created wonderful expressions of deep connection, moments that were special and will be remembered forever.

If you were to give a title to a book about this person and your relationship with them, what would the title be?

DAY 15
NOTHING

It is awfully hard work doing nothing.
—Oscar Wilde

What's wrong with *nothing*?

In grief, *nothing* actually takes a lot of effort.

With emotions and thoughts running high, slowing down and resting is actually a challenge.

Breathing helps a lot. Deep breathing.

Do nothing today because nothing is something that we all we need when we are grieving.

DAY 16
GOODBYE

Since love grows within you, so beauty grows. For love is the beauty of the soul.
—Saint Augustine

GOODBYE IS SUCH a strange word. Is it really *good*? It's especially odd when we use it in reference to a loved one who has died.

When we leave our grandchildren following a visit, we immediately begin to talk about the time we spent together—great stories and memories. We carry those little people with us even though we are no longer in their home. We say "goodbye" with our mouths, but they still remain in our hearts because of what we just experienced.

Do you have to say "goodbye" to someone who has died?

How about including them in your next chapter through memories, stories and the life you shared together?

Wouldn't you rather say "hello" than "goodbye?"

DAY 17
VOICES

The shoe that fits one person pinches another; there is no recipe for living that suits all cases.
—Carl Jung

WHOM DO YOU listen to in your grief journey? Just because someone has gone through a grief journey doesn't make them an expert.

And just because someone writes something about it and puts it on the internet, doesn't mean it's healthy or helpful material.

All information requires discernment.

It's good to hear another person's story and to research a topic, but it doesn't replace asking yourself hard questions. What matters to *you* most? Determine the answer to that question and you may find the answer you need to move forward.

But first you might have to silence the voices so that you can hear yourself think.

DAY 18
BREWING

Emotions are contagious. We've all known it experientially. You know after you have a really fun coffee with a friend, you feel good. When you have a rude clerk in a store, you away feeling bad.
—Daniel Goleman

What's brewing in your life? What's irritating you? A person? A situation? A worry?

Grief wants to take you to places that you've never been before. While you can visit those places, you still need to know that you can leave them behind as well.

DAY 19
COGNITIVE

What we once enjoyed and deeply loved we can never lose, for all that we love deeply becomes a part of us.
—Helen Keller

YOU ARE NOT going crazy. Your mind is very complex and is trying to process all the rapid-fire information that is coming at you.

So much to think about. So many decisions to make. Tons to process.

- Do you seem a little forgetful at times?
- Do you find that making even little decisions is harder than before?
- Are you confused about your future?
- Is it hard for you to concentrate now that you have returned to work?
- Do you find you're worrying about things that you didn't used to worry about?

Go easy on yourself. You *will* make it through. These are normal reactions.

DAY 20
SIPPING

Don't worry about the world coming to an end today. It's already tomorrow in Australia.
—Charles Schulz

BE AWARE OF steps that are too big in your grief journey.

"Too much too soon" can lead to heartache or decisions that you'll regret.

Be patient and kind to yourself and others.

Sipping is always better than gulping.

DAY 21
CURIOUS QUESTION #1

What do you say to *Anxious* when it dominates your thoughts?

THAT PROBABLY SOUNDS like an odd turn of phrase. However, it's actually a really important question. When you take *Anxious* and make it a proper noun, you can have a conversation with it. When you personify it, you can more readily dialogue with it and keep it from taking control of your mind and emotions.

More often than not, there is one thought that tends to dominate your mind when you're grieving. Today we look at *Anxious*:

- What is *Anxious* saying to you that is true? False? How is it limiting you?
- Where will you put *Anxious* in relationship to other areas of your life?
- What needs more attention than *Anxious*?

DAY 22
PHYSICAL

Grief is like the ocean; it comes on waves ebbing and flowing. Sometimes the water is calm, and sometimes it is overwhelming. All we can do is learn to swim.
—Vicki Harrison

Our bodies have a way of letting us know when we're stressed. Don't be surprised by your body's reaction to grief.

It's not uncommon to experience some of the following as a physical reaction to grief:

- Fatigue
- Disrupted sleep patterns
- Heart palpitations
- Skin rash
- Loss of appetite
- Aching muscles
- Migraine headaches

I'm sure you can add to this list.

I wonder if you've had any unexplained aches and pains. If you have, you might want to pay a visit to your family doctor, but don't let it concern you too much. Your body may just be speaking to you about the grief you are experiencing.

DAY 23
NIGHT

True silence is the rest of the mind and is to the spirit what sleep is to the body, nourishment and refreshment.
—WILLIAM PENN

THE LAST THING you take in with your mind before you go to sleep at night is important. What you read, watch, listen to, talk about, and reflect upon will likely impact your sleep.

How do you quiet your mind so that it's not working overtime?

A nighttime grief routine may be important for you to consider.

Do you have one? Maybe it's time.

DAY 24
CAMERA

*It's hard to forget someone who gave
you so much to remember.*
–Unknown

WHO NEEDS A stand-alone camera when you have an iPhone that can take great pictures? An iPhone has auto-focus; a camera has numerous settings that you need to fiddle with. An iPhone does it all for you. Snap! Done! Picture perfect!

Unlike the iPhone, there's no auto-focus in grief. There are so many small adjustments that you are constantly making in life, some of which you may never have even considered before. Is your life a little blurry right now? You're re-focusing and that's hard work.

DAY 25
AIR

*Why does it take a minute to say hello
and forever to say goodbye?*
—Unknown

GRIEF CAN BE suffocating.

I was reminded of this while wearing my medical mask for a long period of time the other day. I wanted so much to take it off, cast it aside and breath in some fresh air.

But I couldn't. Circumstances wouldn't allow it.

In a similar way, you long to "take off" grief, throw it away and breathe easy again.

But right now, you can't.

In time though, you will.

DAY 26
SOCKS

Given a choice between grief and nothing, I'd choose grief.
–William Faulkner

Tube socks are great. I love that they're one-size-fits-all. Because they don't have a heel, there's no need for different sizes to fit various sized feet.

Why then isn't every sock a tube sock? Wouldn't it make sock manufacturing a lot simpler? Why not? Because there's nothing like wearing socks that fit perfectly on your feet. Well-fitted socks make walking and running so much easier.

Grief is never a one-size-fits-all experience. Don't try to fit into another person's way of managing grief.

Your grief is unique because you are unique.

Be patient. Never compare yourself with another. It won't help you in the long run.

DAY 27
EMOTIONS

What soap is for the body, tears are for the soul.
—Jewish proverb

So often, it's difficult to understand why we feel the way we do. Emotions are challenging to manage and can feel like a tangled ball—especially when you are grieving.

I could give you a long list of feelings that accompany grief, but I'm pretty sure you have a long list of your own. No doubt you do—someone dear to you has died.

Is there a particular emotion that is weighing you down in your grief journey at the moment? That's a question I would ask myself in my own grief journey. Then I would sit with it and ask further questions.

1. What is its root cause?
2. How did it start and why?
3. If I let it go unchecked, where will it lead me?
4. What options do I have to deal with it so that it doesn't take me off course?

Questions help us sort out our emotions so we can get a handle on how to manage them.

DAY 28
DESTINTATION

Only people who are capable of loving strongly can also suffer great sorrow, but this same necessity of loving serves to counteract their grief and heals them.
—Leo Tolstoy

There's no final destination in grief. It's a milk run with lots of stops and no end.

Actually, it's comprised of beginnings and transitions. This is important to know. We must resist the erroneous notion that grief has a finish line.

That may sound ominous, but it's not something to be afraid of. The person who has died will always have a place in your life even if they are no longer physically present.

When you miss them in the future—and grief returns—remember what it is that they left you with and cherish that. There is something good that has become part of your life forever.

DAY 29
JUMP

These days grief seems like walking on a frozen river; most of the time he feels safe enough, but there is always that danger he will plunge through.
—David Nicholls, One Day

"Jump and I will catch you. Don't worry. I won't miss. I promise."

It was hard to get those grandchildren to jump into the water for the first time. Even if Grandpa was in the water close by and ready to catch them, they were still hesitant.

Of course, I've got a history of jumping into water over my head and I can swim, but they were young and just learning, so they were a little more cautious.

Everything is difficult the first time. If you've previously experienced grief, you understand this. You know you'll be OK. But if you haven't ever experienced grief, you're likely more tentative or fearful about what's next.

It's not easy to jump into deep areas that are uncomfortable.

Is there someone whom you can count on to catch you if you've jumped into the deep end of your grief?

DAY 30
EMBERS

When it is darkest, we can see the stars.
—Ralph Waldo Emerson

"Start with the kindling first. The fire will catch that and then you can add bigger logs to the fire," I said to my grandkids. It's tempting to throw a big log onto the fire right away, hoping that it will ignite. It's a lot more work to find small twigs or take an axe and make kindling that will get the fire going.

It's the same with grief. Work through "smaller pieces" of your grief at the beginning. It's a lot easier than trying to tackle the big issues that weigh you down and risk "putting out your fire."

Those embers? They're still burning deep within. You may not feel very alive right now, but that's OK. Your passion for life will ignite again—but it all starts with a little kindling, my friend.

DAY 31
FORWARD

Life begins at the end of your comfort zone.
—Neale Donald Walsch

I WONDER IF IT drives you crazy to hear this sentence: "You need to move forward with your life." People assume that just because you talk about the person who has died or have not entered into life as fully as you did before, that you are not "going about grief" the right way.

What is the *right way*? Can your life be exactly as it was before? I don't believe so.

Grief is more than an interruption—it has turned your life upside down. The road you had planned on taking has changed. This is difficult because you had some plans moving forward and now you are forced to rethink or reimagine your future.

One step at a time. Your path forward will change. And there will be some forks, but you will figure it out—at your own pace.

DAY 32
STAGES

I always like to look on the optimistic side of life, but I am realistic enough to know that life is a complex matter.
—Walt Disney

Please don't get caught up in the "stages of grief"—a term we hear so frequently.

There is no such thing as a linear experience in grief—one that you walk through and emerge from on the other side to experience new life following death.

Grief is messy and doesn't follow an order. There is no finish line.

There's no check list in the grief experience, nothing that will help you move through it in an orderly fashion.

Grief twists and turns. It's far from having neat, tidy categories. It's a bumpy road and takes time.

DAY 33
SING

Overall, social singing is linked to a number of health advantages including social bonding with others, happiness, diminished stress, better immune function, and better sleep.
—Dr. Stuart MacDonald

I noticed the CD on the store shelf. It was an album I used to listen to as a teenager. It reminded me of special memories from my past—especially one song that was my all-time favourite.

Music comes in the back door of memory and brings people and experiences back into our life in a flash. Through it, we can visualize the person, feel the feeling, and remember the event or story associated with that song.

Take some time today to play a special song that was important for you and the person who died.

Listen to the music, cherish the relationship and sing along at the top of your lungs.

DAY 34
BRAIN

Even if I knew that tomorrow the world would go to pieces, I would still plant my apple tree.
—Martin Luther

Our brains are exceedingly complex, processing upwards of eleven million pieces of information every second. That's a crazy amount of information.

Add to that the stress of numerous "smaller" losses that surround the huge loss of someone dying in your life, and you have a mind that is overloaded.

It stands to reason that whatever you're focussing on is going to take up the most cognitive real estate in your brain. Perhaps there are other things that need your attention, but they're not being given any space because of the one thing that keeps nagging at you.

What's the reoccurring or challenging thought that comes to mind this very moment? Write it down. You can either choose to release that recurring thought (if it's something over which you have no control) or take action to deal with it.

Either way, do one thing that will change your situation and free up some neurons.

DAY 35
SIT

Tears water our growth.
–WILLIAM SHAKESPEARE

SOMETIMES I LIKE to just sit and ponder, doing nothing except looking out the window with no purpose but to take in whatever is in front of me. At times I'm not even sure what I'm supposed to be taking in—maybe that's OK.

I have not always been good at *doing nothing,* but I've seen how beneficial it can be when I just sit.

My *sitting* is not usually intentional or premeditated. Oddly when I do nothing, I'm actually doing something—I'm giving space for something to come that I had not planned for or expected.

Perhaps that's a little like meditation. Quiet your mind and heart.

What are you hearing in the silence?

DAY 36
TEAM

Every human being must have boundaries in order to have successful relationships or a successful performance in life.
—Henry Cloud

I ENJOY SPORTS—PARTICULARLY TEAM sports.
There are so many lessons I've learned by being involved in athletics—lessons I've carried with me throughout my life.

The most important thing for me has been learning how to work together as a team to achieve a goal.

A person might be a super athlete, but if they don't know how to collaborate, the likelihood of success or even having fun is slim to none.

Grief too has to be played in the context of team. Your grief is greatly impacted by those closest to you, your team. Inviting them to come alongside you in your grief experience is something worth considering.

DAY 37
GUILT

Forgiveness must be immediate, whether or not a person asks for it. Trust must be rebuilt over time. Trust requires a track record.
—RICK WARREN

GUILT IS FEELING badly about what you have done (or wished you had done but didn't) as you look back and examine your relationship with the person who has died.

Guilt is part of most people's grief journey and an overarching theme in the human experience in general. We all fail each other to some degree because we are not perfect. And we feel badly about that, even if we don't say it out loud.

Being honest about your shortcomings and learning to forgive yourself is an important movement forward as you miss someone.

What do you think your loved one would answer in response to your *I'm sorry*?

More likely than not, they would release you from whatever was keeping you bound. They would want to set you free to move forward in life and experience what was next.

DAY 38
STRANGER

It's a wonderful thing to be optimistic. It keeps you healthy and it keeps you resilient.
—Daniel Kahneman

Have you ever stopped and visited with a stranger only to discover that you have a lot in common? You may never have met them before, but because you took the time to engage them in conversation, you feel like you know them now—and it surprises you.

Grief is like a stranger at first.

As you begin to take the time to engage Grief, you discover that it wants a deeper relationship with you.

That probably sounds very odd. But there is something powerful about befriending your grief so that it's beside you—outside of yourself—and you can *talk* to it in a different way without being held hostage by it.

DAY 39
AVALANCHE

I am a slow walker, but I never walk back.
–Abraham Lincoln

THE SIGN SAID, "Avalanche Area. Slow Down!" I have to admit, I began looking nervously at the mountainous cliffs on either side of the road as I drove through them in my car.

"What are the chances?" I asked myself. I guess it must happen. But the sign said to slow down? I thought, "Why slow down? Don't I want to get *ahead* of any potential avalanche!"

Can you outdrive an avalanche? Probably not. "Just keep driving, Rick," I said to myself, clutching the steering wheel.

In grief, it's easy to worry about a potential emotion or event *snowing you under* and *doing you in*. With fresh grief especially, there are a lot of things happening and you wonder how to get ahead of them.

You can't. They'll catch up. Just keep driving.

DAY 40
FORGET

*When someone you love becomes a memory,
the memory becomes a treasure.*
—Unknown

You don't have to forget a loved one in order to move on with your life. Forgetting or ignoring can be detrimental to your healing in the grief journey.

What's important is that you create an enduring connection with the person you loved (and still love). How you remember them is up to you. But the more intentional you are about celebrating the relationship you had, the better it will be for you in the long run.

Grief will bring this person back—but think through how you might relate to them when it does. If you do, it will help you manage the kind of grief that *takes you out* when you're least prepared.

DAY 41
LOVE

We were promised sufferings. They were part of the program. We were even told, "Blessed are they that mourn," and I accept it. I've got nothing that I hadn't bargained for. Of course, it is different when the thing happens to oneself, not to others and in reality, not imagination.
           –C. S. Lewis

My friend said, "I was about to enter the flower shop but stopped in my tracks. I thought I'd pick up something for my wife for Valentine's Day. Then I realized—she's not with me this year. And I cried."

"Why did you stop?" I asked.

It's okay to do something you used to do for your loved one—even if they are no longer here.

You still love this person. Maybe doing something that brings back memories of them on an anniversary, birthday or special occasion is a good idea.

DAY 42
CURIOUS QUESTION #2

What do you do with *Frightened* when it creeps into your thinking about the future?

WORRYING ABOUT THE future is a common struggle when someone dear to you dies. Even if you don't want to go there, you fear what's next without this person in your life. It's too difficult to imagine living day-to-day without them.

Frightened wants to take you to places that are not real. It wants you to imagine a scary or sad future. It gets you all stirred up.

Today, make a decision to live in this present day and not dwell on future scenarios. Eventually *Frightened* will give up—perhaps even go away entirely.

Where will you place *Frightened* today so that it's not so troublesome?

DAY 43
AFTER

People touch our lives if only for a moment, and yet we're not the same from that moment on. The time is not important. The moment is forever.
—Fern Bork

THE DAY AFTER. Do you remember the day after your loved one died?

I do. It was awful.

Reality set in quickly. I cried a lot.

Why? Because I missed my wife and knew that my life would never be the same again.

Did I want that? No. It wasn't my choice.

My choice was to find joy again.

And that took some time. But I finally did.

DAY 44
CELEBRATIONS

Those we love don't go away, they walk beside us every day… unseen, unheard, but always near, still loved, still missed, and very dear.
—Unknown

Families gather to celebrate—but there's an empty chair. Someone used to sit in it, but they're gone now. Amid the tinsel, the presents, the reunion of family, and the great food, there is missing. There are mixed emotions that need to be acknowledged.

Many of us have strong family traditions during the holidays. Have some of these changed because your loved one isn't there this year?

Rather than changing your traditions, you may want to consider intentionally adding a new family tradition in order to honor that missing family member.

DAY 45
ROOM

We need never be afraid of our tears.
—Charles Dickens

I'M NOT SURE that I want to make room for you in my life, Grief. You're not exactly pleasant. You bring me sadness, tears and even anger. I know that I need to give you space, but I can't give you too much.

I have other rooms in my life that I need to visit. I'll open the door to you when I'm ready.

But I'll also close it when I need to.

DAY 46
SPINNING

*Above all else, guard your heart, for
everything you do flows from it.*
—King Solomon

Did you ever play with a spinning top when you were a kid? You know, the kind where you push the lever up and down and it spins and spins, lights flashing as it goes?

When we lose someone dear to us, grief has a way of making negative thoughts spin over and over in our minds. We don't want to obsess over these thoughts but can't seem to help it. At some level, we hope that by dwelling on an event, an idea, a memory or an emotion that it will be resolved.

This spinning in grief can also become a downward spiral unless we take control of the thought, stop giving it airtime and replace it with another that is more positive.

Exchanging a compulsive thought for one that brings you peace is a good idea—it will keep you from spinning.

DAY 47
BONDS

*Find a place inside where there's joy, and
the joy will burn out the pain.*
—Joseph Campbell

Continuing bonds—they remind us of stories about our loved one and help us feel connected to them.

Do you have special items that remind you of this person? Did you go fishing together? Maybe you have a fishing rod that connects you. Were you given something of theirs that was important to you? What did you do together? What about the places you visited or hung out together? What activities did you share?

What moments bring you joy when you think about this person? Return to those when you need to feel connected to that person again.

DAY 48
CONTAGIOUS

We bereaved are not alone. We belong to the largest company in all the world—the company of those who have known suffering.
—HELEN KELLER

WASH YOUR HANDS often. Sneeze or cough into your elbow. Don't touch your face. Keep your social distance. Wear your mask. We all got used to these mantras that began in 2020. They were ways to help control the spread of COVID-19.

Some people act as if grief is contagious, keeping away from those who are grieving. But grief can't and shouldn't be lived out in isolation.

Grieving people need your caring presence. Connect with them. They'll always be grateful for it.

DAY 49
REASON

Here is a test to find whether your mission on Earth is finished: If you're alive, it isn't.
—Richard Bach

There is not a reason for everything that happens in your life. Contrary to popular belief, science can't always help you figure out everything you need to know in order to experience peace.

It does not have all the answers, especially when it comes to grief. It can tell you all about the neurotransmitters in your brain, but it can't solve your grief.

We are complicated beings and aren't easily "figured out." Maybe grief has more to do with mystery than we realize.

Perhaps *mystery* can speak to us about our grief.

DAY 50
RHYTHM

Have patience with all things. But first of all, with yourself.
—Saint Francis de Sales

There is very little rhythm in life when you are grieving. Everything is out of sync. The tempo feels all wrong. The beat, irregular.

Any attempt to jump back into life seems to be met with resistance—from within and from without.

Be careful not to move too fast.

You can't pick up the pace in your grief journey. Take it easy.

The rhythm will return in good time.

DAY 51
FREE

We've shared our lives these many years. You've held my hand; you've held my heart. So many blessings, so few tears—yet for a moment, we must part.
—Unknown

Who doesn't like a good deal? It feels good not to pay full price for an item, doesn't it? You bring it home and exclaim, "Look what I got—it was on sale!" But you still had to pay *something* for it. It wasn't free.

No one gets a free ride in grief.

We wish we could because it hurts, but there is a price for grief. Do you know what it is? LOVE.

Because you loved that person, the grief hurts all the more.

That's the price you pay for grief. But it's not such a bad deal. Loss means you loved.

DAY 52
CHEERLEADER

I never said I worship her, I just said I'm very fond of the ground on which she walks!
–Linus Van Pelt, Peanuts

EVERYONE NEEDS A cheerleader in their life. A child looks for her parents in the stands at a sporting event or in the auditorium at a school play. She needs to know that her *cheerleaders* are there for her.

In grief, I believe we need cheering on too. Cheerleaders are those who are closet to us and believe in us. This is not about cheering *up*—it's about cheering *on*.

Sometimes the person who died has been your cheerleader and you're likely missing their encouraging words. You counted on them.

But now the question is, "How might the person who died be cheering you on in your next steps?" I'm almost positive you can hear their words and know exactly what they might be saying to you today.

DAY 53
CHECK-IN

Grief is like the ocean; it comes on waves ebbing and flowing. Sometimes the water is calm, and sometimes it is overwhelming. All we can do is learn to swim.
—Vicki Harrison

There are certain things you're not allowed to bring through security when you're at the airport. Yet I'm always amazed at the line-up of people whose bags contain forbidden items—water bottles, scissors, jars of jam, knitting needles, pocketknives. I guess people just forget to verify what's in their carry-on luggage before they check in at the airport.

We also need to be careful what we bring with us on our grief journey. Leaving some things behind is important in order to grieve well.

What should be left behind? That depends. Only you know what brings you down. Check in with yourself at the beginning of each day. Keep the good stuff and let the rest go.

DAY 54
END

There are some who bring a light so great to the world that even after they have gone the light remains.
—Unknown

THE END.
Is it really? The end of a person's life on earth has finished but your relationship with them has not.

No doubt, the relationship is different. It has to be.

But you have the choice to include them into your next chapter. Remember, they're already part of your life by virtue of the time you spent together.

So, invite them to help you find a new beginning.

DAY 55
ISOLATION

Love, and do what you like.
—Saint Augustine

You are not alone.

You need people in your life during your grief journey. Of course, you need time alone as well. But those who have an authentic and caring community are able to transition in their life and discover what's next more easily than those who don't have a community. Research affirms this fact.

Isolation is hard on us. Don't try to *go it alone* when you are grieving. Come out and find human connection with family and friends.

Reach out and find a community where you feel you can belong. Open up to someone who cares and listens to your heart.

There are good people in the world who are waiting to come alongside you.

DAY 56
ANNIVERSARY

Traditions are our roots and a profile of who we are as individuals and who we are as a family. They are our roots, which give us stability and a sense of belonging. They ground us.
—Lidia Bastianich

THE ANNIVERSARY OF a loved one's death is always a difficult day.

Strong memories encircle our hearts and minds as we think about the love that was shared.

So why not gather as a family and remember? Yes, there will be some tears as you miss that person, but what else might be shared? How will you remember? What about…

- going to her place of burial with flowers?
- cooking his favourite meal?
- singing her favourite song?
- sharing a story about them?
- giving a gift in his memory?
- looking through the family photo albums together?

- taking out an item of theirs and talking about its significance?
- celebrating him the best way you can by bringing him closer to you?

DAY 57
WEEKEND

Sometimes all you can do is hug a friend tightly and wish that their pain could be transferred by touch to your own emotional hard drive.
—Richelle E. Goodrich

WHY ARE THE weekends so hard for so many grieving people?

I keep hearing people say, "Weekends are hard because that was our time to connect, to do special things together, to visit family and friends, to enjoy our leisure activities together."

DAY 58
MEANING

Grief opens a place in our hearts that we never knew could hurt so profoundly, but it also opens this same place to a love we never imagined possible.
—U<small>NKNOWN</small>

"M<small>EANING</small>"—<small>SUCH A BIG</small> word and especially important in the days that follow loss.

As you step forward in your grief journey, death will push you into some very deep thinking. Why? Because when you grieve, you're not just thinking about your loved one's death, but your own mortality as well—if you're honest with yourself at least.

Death drives each of us to re-think and re-prioritize our lives. We think about the person who has died. Then we think about our own life and what we want out of it.

"What is the most important thing in my life?" Your grief journey will help you answer that as you think about the meaning of life…your life.

DAY 59
LADDER

There is a sacredness in tears. They are not the mark of weakness, but of power. They speak more eloquently than ten thousand tongues. They are the messengers of overwhelming grief, of deep contrition, and of unspeakable love.
—Washington Irving

He was carrying a ladder under his arm as he walked down the street. I wondered where he was going. Wherever it was, he needed to reach for a very high spot given the size of the ladder.

Grief forces us to reach. It makes us climb higher and see things we hadn't seen before and discover resources we didn't know we had.

Need a ladder?

DAY 60
HEARTACHE

When we lose someone we love, we must learn not to live without them, but to live with the love they left behind.
—Unknown

One day at a time.

That's how you feel when you miss someone who has died.

You wonder how you could possibly make it through the day with the weight of grief that you carry—the heartache that you are experiencing.

You cannot fill the heart-space that belongs to someone who has died. The love you shared, the time you spent together, the relationship you had with that person—there were all significant and deserve to have a place in your heart—forever.

You do have a big heart. There's always room for more love. For new love.

It's okay to keep on loving. And remembering.

DAY 61
SWING

F-E-A-R has two meanings: "Forget Everything and Run" or "Face Everything and Rise." The choice is yours.
—Zig Ziglar

"Give me a push, Grandpa!" the grandkids ask when I go to the park with them. They all want a push at the same time it seems. So, I go from swing to swing until each of them sails skyward on their own.

Do you remember going to the playground as a kid? It was challenging to swing really high by yourself, wasn't it? Sure, you could pump your legs to get going, but it was so much easier when someone else gave you a push.

We all need a push. We need people to come alongside us in our grief. People to cheer us on and to hear our deepest thoughts and hold us when necessary.

But we also have to learn to swing on our own. Both are necessary.

DAY 62
MONDAY

*Learn from yesterday, live for today, look
to tomorrow, rest this afternoon.*
—Charles Schulz

For most of us, Monday means the beginning of a new week.

If we've been fortunate, we've taken a Sabbath to rest and feel refreshed.

Unfortunately, grief does not take a Sabbath.

But you can make choices that prevent grief from depleting you of rest or sapping your energy.

Find that thing that brings rest to your being.

You need it.

DAY 63
CURIOUS QUESTION #3

Who in your family needs you most right now?

GRIEF IS SELF-CENTERED. Why? Because grief is personal. It reflects the relationship you had with the person who has died–this is YOUR grief.

On the flipside, there are others who are also missing this person. They are sharing the same grief journey with you, but in a different way. So, it looks and feels different.

Because grief takes you into a place of deep self-conversation, it may be difficult to notice how *others* are doing. You might want to check in with those around you who are also missing this person.

Is there someone you are concerned about right now?

DAY 64
BENCH

Life Lesson 3: You can't rush grief. It has its own timetable. All you can do is make sure there are lots of soft places around—beds, pillows, arms, laps.
–Patti Davis

I'm always grateful when I go for a hike and see a bench up ahead. It means I can rest for a bit before continuing on.

Where do you rest in your grief journey? Grief is hard work. There is no way for it not to tire you, even exhaust you at times.

Grief work is just as tiring as physical work—if not more so. You have to slow down so that your heart and mind can rest—there is so much transition taking place on so many levels.

Where do you sit for a while just to embrace your grief and ask yourself questions?

Find a bench where you can converse with your grieving heart before starting again on the next leg of your journey. You'll be glad you rested.

DAY 65
ELASTIC

Grieving is a necessary passage and a difficult transition to finally letting go of sorrow—it is not a permanent rest stop.
—Dodinsky

GRIEF IS MUCH like an elastic band. Tension and release.

You're pulled between two things. You want to stay where you are and remember life with your loved one. But then life, by its very nature, begins to move you forward. The elastic is stretched between *what used to be* and *what is now* or *what could be*. You're afraid it (or you) might snap as you're pulled in two directions.

Ever feel that way? Afraid to move forward? The tension does release when you give up a little of the past and embrace the future. You might be surprised how relieved you feel.

DAY 66
DILUTE

Experience is a hard teacher because she gives the test first, the lesson afterward.
—Vernon Law

COFFEE THAT'S WEAK in its flavour is not enjoyable to drink. Lemonade that's been watered down just doesn't do it for me. A soft drink that's mostly water is just gross. At least that's my take on drinks that are diluted.

Same goes for a grief experience—it shouldn't be diluted. It's too rich and important and will shape who you become. Don't walk away from it or add stuff to it so that you don't feel the pain. If you do, you may miss out on something that's important for you in your next chapter. Just keep asking, "What's your message to me, Grief? I want to know; I want to learn."

It might seem odd to stay in grief when it's so hard but leaving too soon can actually make it harder in the end. There's work to do before you can move forward. Deep, authentic work.

There is only one way to tackle grief—that's right in the middle of it.

DAY 67
PERFECT

If you love, you will grieve, and that's just given.
—Kay Redfield Jamison

No relationship is (or was) perfect. We are human beings, and all live with regrets to some degree.

In grief, we automatically think about the life we had with the person who is no longer physically present. We think about stories and events. We examine our relationship with this person.

And sometimes, we tend to think it was not enough. It could have been different. I could have said more. I could have spent more time with them.

We are hard on ourselves and forget that no relationship is ever perfect—you with them and they with you.

The quicker we learn that the easier it will be to celebrate what was and is now.

DAY 68
PROTECTION

Grief never ends but it changes. It's a passage not a place to stay. Grief is not a sign of weakness, nor a lack of faith. It is the price of love.
—Unknown

I love watching turtles. They tuck their heads under their hard shell to protect themselves from perceived harm.

It's equally fun to see them pop their little heads, neck and feet back out once they feel safe again. Then they continue their lumbering journey forward.

In grief, protection is important. Protect your boundaries. Protect your mind. Protect your health.

But especially protect your heart. It's very fragile.

While it's important to share from your heart at times, it's also crucial to know when to "tuck it in" and protect it. It's crucial actually.

You will learn what works for you—you'll know because your heart will tell you.

Listen carefully to your heart.

DAY 69
MOST

At the blueness of the skies and in the warmth of summer, we remember them.
—Sylvan Kamens & Rabbi Jack Reimer

Sharing stories about your loved one with other people is important. Maybe today you want to share your most memorable moments of the person whom you're missing.

What are some of the stories of connection for which you are most grateful? Why not share one of these stories with another person? You can start with, "Today I remembered this special story about _____ and I wanted to share it with you."

This is especially important in fresh grief when you'd rather move on—but don't do it. Tell a story instead.

DAY 70
BLUE CHEESE

Only people who are capable of loving strongly can also suffer great sorrow, but this same necessity of loving serves to counteract their grief and heals them.
—Leo Tolstoy

For years, I hated the taste of blue cheese. Actually, I think it was the pungent smell that turned me off.

But recently, I gave it another shot. Now I can't get enough of it.

Don't you find it interesting that the very thing that irritated you about the person who is no longer living, is the very thing you miss the most right now?

The way they used to leave their dirty socks on the floor, or forget to screw the lids on containers, or snored at night?

Yes, they made that person unique. Those things used to bug you, but now you wish your person was still around to do those irritating things.

It's ironic, isn't it?

DAY 71
UNIQUE

Always remember that you are absolutely unique. Just like everyone else.
—Margaret Mead

EACH OF US is unique and will approach our grief journey differently. This is stating the obvious, I realize. But why do we each have a unique perspective on our grief? What accounts for those differences?

Have you ever taken a hard look at your grief history? Where have you learned about grief? Where has your *grief education* come from? How did your family *do grief* when you were growing up? Did they talk openly or keep silent about the one who died? Did they remove all reminders of that person or honour their memory?

Your perspective comes from somewhere. It might be time to examine your *database* of grief experiences and ask if it's meeting your needs.

DAY 72
HIDE

Grief is not a disorder, a disease or a sign of weakness. It is an emotional, physical and spiritual necessity, the price you pay for love. The only cure for grief is to grieve.
—Earl Grollman

As a child, I loved playing hide and seek. Now as a grandpa, I get to play it again. When the grandkids were infants, it began as a game of peek-a-boo. But they're older now so hide-and-seek has evolved into all-out war and complex hiding spots.

Sometimes, the one who is hiding does such a great job that we have to call out, "I can't find you! I give up!" Then they emerge from their creative hiding place.

Grief wants you to hide and not be found. It isolates you.

That's why it's important to have people around you who check up on you regularly—family or friends who can find you if hiding becomes an obsession for you.

It's good to be found once in a while.

DAY 73
BATTLE

You're never going to kill storytelling, because it's built into the human plan. We come with it.
—Margaret Atwood

SOMETIMES PEOPLE REFER to grief as a battle.

If the relationship with the person who died was a challenging one, the memories can be difficult when they return.

But for the most part, grief is not an enemy. Why is that? If grief means missing someone you love, how could grief be an enemy?

Grief is bringing back someone whom you love and always will.

Instead of battling against grief when it returns, why not welcome it as an opportunity to reflect upon what you miss? What was special to you about that person who died? Savor those things.

We remember for a reason, because that relationship was important to us.

When grief returns, honor it—it's bringing back something important to you—the person whom you still love.

DAY 74
DESCRIBE

No one ever told me that grief felt so like fear.
—C.S. Lewis

"Grief is like..."

People use so many interesting metaphors and similes to describe their grief. It reminds me how each person deals with grief uniquely. Even the language we use to talk about grief varies from person to person.

"Grief is like a roller coaster that you can't get off of."

How do *you* describe grief?

DAY 75
COKE

Our grief is as individual as our lives.
—Elisabeth Kübler-Ross

Coke or Pepsi? It's a choice. A preference.
You have a grieving preference as well, a unique way of processing grief that is different from other people. Be careful when others tell you how you should grief.

They might point out what *they* have done based on their experience and think that it's a one-size-fits-all scenario. There might be some similarities with their experience and yours, but you are unique. Your life journey is different from theirs.

Learn from others but take time to discover your own grief way.

It's the only one that is right for you.

DAY 76
BULLDOZER

*Whenever I feel really alone, I just sit
and stare into the night sky.*
—Charlie Brown, Peanuts

Does everything feel heavy right now? People? Work? Routine? Getting up in the morning?

You're doing your best to move forward with your life, but it's tough slogging. You are just trying to press on with everything that's on your plate. Head down and bulldoze forward. Is this you right now?

Some of the heavy tasks of grief *will* go away, but in the meantime, you may need to cut yourself and others some slack.

DAY 77
ANGER

*Anger is an acid that can do more harm
to the vessel in which it is stored than to
anything on which it is poured.*
—Mark Twain

Anger is a common—and fair—reaction to grief. It's one that requires attention.

Why is that? Because anger can harm relationships and cause further pain both to yourself and others.

Your response to grief is never only about you. Anger often pushes you in a direction that's not healthy or productive.

Take a close look at anger when it surfaces and ask why it's there and how much time you plan to give it in your day.

DAY 78
RIDE

You may delay, but time will not.
—Benjamin Franklin

I SAW THE OLD cars driving down the road. Such classics. "Must be going to a show," I said to my wife. "What was your first car?" she asked me. "A 1977 Monte Carlo," I replied. I drove it for six months. As a poor college student, I couldn't afford the gas, so traded it up for a Pontiac Astre station wagon.

The ride is so different for each of us on the grief journey. As soon as I think I've "heard it all" in my thirty-five years of counseling people in their grief, I hear someone share something about their grief that is unique.

Your grief journey will be like no other. But you will have to *drive* it in the direction it needs to go.

DAY 79
FOREVER

You don't go around grieving all the time, but the grief is still there and always will be.
—NIGELLA LAWSON

You: How long will my grief last?

Rick: Forever.

You: That doesn't sound very comforting!

Rick: Do you think you will always miss the person who died?

You: Yes.

Rick: So, if grief returns at different times in your life, it only means that you miss that person. You cherish what was special about your relationship with them—a relationship that lasts forever. What's wrong with that?

You: Nothing. So, I'll miss them forever?

Rick: That's exactly right.

DAY 80
MOMENTS

*When we have joy we crave to
share; We remember them.*
—Sylvan Kamens & Rabbi Jack Riemer

He said, "I wish I could have spoken to him just one more time." His friend had died of a Fentanyl overdose.

"It's so unfair," he said. I nodded in agreement. "I just wish I had had more moments with him," he continued. "You must have really cared about him," I said. He stopped and looked at me. "He was my best friend," he said.

"Tell me a story about you and your best friend," I said.

And he began. He'd had many wonderful moments with his friend but because he was fresh in his grief, he could only remember what he *no longer* had.

By the time we left each other that morning, he remembered what he *did* have—never enough but still a lot.

DAY 81
SORRY

A ton of regret never makes an ounce of difference.
–Grenville Kleiser, Dictionary of Proverbs

How do you say, "I'm sorry," to someone who has died?

We all have words we wished we had said before our loved one died—words that remained inside our hearts but never made it beyond our thoughts. It's tough to have those residual, unspoken words lingering in the mind.

I frequently hear clients say, "I wish I had said that I was sorry for…"

Even by having those feelings and those regrets, you are saying something very important. The words *I'm sorry* actually show that you do love and care. Otherwise, it wouldn't matter to you.

So, don't be hard on yourself. Focus on the important thing—not on what you didn't have but what you did have.

DAY 82
TRAFFIC

The most beautiful people we have known are those who have known defeat, known suffering, known struggle, known loss, and have found their way out of those depths.

—Elisabeth Kübler-Ross

WHERE ARE THE passengers in all those vehicles? There are so many cars with just one driver—no one else in the passenger seat beside them. Cars, trucks, SUVs—bumper to bumper, heading down the highway and only one person in them—the driver. All alone.

Are you all alone on your grief journey? Don't drive it by yourself.

Take someone along on the journey. The HOV lane will get you where you want to go more quickly anyway.

DAY 83
WAVES

I love you for giving me your eyes, for staying back and watching me shine.
–Taylor Swift

I LOVE WADING OUT into the ocean's waves. Once in a while though, a wave catches me by surprise and pulls me out further than I had planned, and it scares me a little.

Grief can be like a rogue wave whose vortex pulls you beyond your comfort zone until you feel out of control.

But if you didn't venture out into the ocean, you would also miss out on experiences that you enjoy, like swimming, riding a wave, surfing, paddle boarding or snorkeling.

Wherever you go in loss, you'll be taking grief with you. That's just the way it is. May as well befriend it—it won't swallow you.

DAY 84
CURIOUS QUESTION #4

**What do you do with *Doubt* when
it takes away your hope?**

*D*OUBT IS A common response to grief. It wants to rob you of your hope. It wants to make you cynical about life. It locks you into a downward spiral and tells you lies about reality.

Has *Doubt* been plaguing you? If yes, where is it taking you that is not real? Where is it taking you so that you are not experiencing hope?

What would you like to say to *Doubt* right now in order to diminish its negative impact on you?

DAY 85
RAINBOWS

Have a nice day. If you are already having a nice day, please disregard this notice.
–Ziggy

Rainbows—I love watching for them. It's the place where rain and light meet.

Dark clouds, rain and sunshine combine to create vibrant colors as the light shines through water droplets.

There are so many colors and shades in grief—including grey. It often feels as though things will remain grey in life.

But the sun needs the rain and the dark clouds in order to create one of the most spectacular and colorful phenomena on earth—the rainbow.

Grief looks and feels drab and gloomy. But watch for those glimpses of light that shine in your rainstorm, creating something vibrant.

DAY 86
JEALOUSY

There is nothing more attractive than a nice smile.
–CHARLES SCHULZ

IF I'M HONEST with myself, I'd say that there were times when I was jealous. I envied those whose loved ones had survived cancer. My first wife didn't.

This was especially true just following her death, when my grief was so fresh.

I would think, "Why me? Why Pam? It's just not fair."

And then I regrouped. Should I not be happy for those who are survivors and celebrate with them? They wouldn't have to experience the sadness that I was experiencing. They would be blessed to spend more time with someone they loved.

And my heart changed—at least a little.

DAY 87
CABIN

When a relationship of love is disrupted, the relationship does not cease. The love continues; therefore, the relationship continues. The work of grief is to reconcile and redeem life to a different love relationship.
—W. Scott Lineberry

WE ALL HAVE them. Our lives are made up of significant stories. You know, the ones that always begin with "remember when?"

Why do we keep sharing them over and over again? Because these stories connect us with our loved one and remind us of a relationship that was a big part of our own narrative.

Our cabin is filled with stories about Pam, a mom who died and is still loved.

What stories connect you to your loved one?

DAY 88
ACCOUNTABILITY

You cannot prevent the birds of sorrow from flying over your head, but you can prevent them from building nests in your hair.
—Old Chinese proverb

When you grieve, you can't think clearly. It's impossible.

Loss of any kind causes elevated cortisol levels in our brains, which results in brain fog. It's a real thing. It's normal.

That's why it's important to check in with close friends and ask them to keep you accountable. Give them permission to speak into your life to let you know what they're seeing.

A good friend who is honest with you is worth their weight in gold.

DAY 89
SALT

Let your hopes, not your hurts, shape your future.
–Robert H. Schuller

SALT HAS HEALING properties, but if you apply it to an open wound, it'll really sting—at least initially.

Grief often feels like an open wound following a loss. The days after the death of someone special are difficult and sting us to the core of our being. As we engage the world and other people around us, our loss seems that much more intense.

But there is something that can help. There is a certain healing property in remembering and sharing the story of the person you miss. It might sting at first, but as you do, the wound will start to heal.

DAY 90
TOUCH

Touch comes before sight, before speech. It is the first language, and the last, and it will always tell the truth.
—Margaret Atwood

For a long time, researchers believed that touch—the most intimate of our senses—was powerful in the moment but would fade quickly from our short-term memory. But a recent study challenges this notion. Findings show that the sense of touch generates memories that are far more complex and longer lasting than previously believed.

As someone whose love language is physical touch, I find it to be one of the most powerful memory connectors for me personally.

Does the way someone touched you, hugged you, or held you hold memories of deep connection for you?

DAY 91
KICK

The secret of getting ahead is getting started.
—Mark Twain

When I kick a soccer ball, it doesn't always go where I want it to. In fact, more often than not, it seems to follow its own trajectory!

Once in a while, my foot meets that ball, and it goes exactly where I want it to go—either into the net or to the person I am trying to pass it to. It feels so good.

It's nice to have a few victories in our grief journey too. It encourages us and helps us to know that we are going to be okay.

DAY 92
FENCE

Grief is a most peculiar thing; we're so helpless in the face of it. It's like a window that will simply open of its own accord. The room grows cold, and we can do nothing but shiver. But it opens a little less each time, and a little less; and one day we wonder what has become of it.
—Arthur Golden

The phrase "sitting on the fence" means no decision has been made yet. You are not sure what's next or what steps you need to take. It's frustrating for you to be on the fence for too long. Why? Because when you lack movement you risk getting stuck. Or that's what people tell you anyway.

Grief tends to force us to sit more than we are accustomed to—and that's actually okay. Making decisions about our future requires space, time and some fence-sitting.

Maybe you need to be okay about sitting on the fence for the time being. Don't let anyone else tell you to get off the fence and start moving.

Slow grief is better than fast grief.

DAY 93
INSPIRATION

We first make our habits, and then our habits make us.
–John Dryden

People are inspired by those who have overcome difficult circumstances. I think every person who has moved through grief and discovered a different life (while still honoring the person whom they miss) is inspirational to me.

I have met many of them in my work as a grief counsellor.

Working through grief is courageous work—but if you try to move around it or ignore it, I can assure you, it will become harder to manage.

Have courage. You can do this.

DAY 94
INTEGRATION

Death leaves a heartache no one can heal;
love leaves a memory no one can steal.
   –Headstone found in Ireland

It's my son's birthday tomorrow.
   I wonder what he'll remember about me after I die. What do I want to be remembered for?
   Think about the one who died—did they leave you with something special.
   What was it?
   What did you learn from them?
   What wisdom did you glean from their life?
   Integrate this person into your story as you move forward, taking with you what was most significant in your relationship with them.

DAY 95
TASTE

The pain passes, but the beauty remains.
–Henri Matisse

MOST PEOPLE'S CULINARY experiences happen with friends or family. So, it makes sense that the food we eat is linked to the people who once sat at our kitchen table, in the backyard around the campfire or at the picnic table.

In many families, there are certain foods that have become traditions and family favorites. Perhaps there's even a family ritual surrounding those dishes.

As you move through your grief journey, you may want to think about what meals were shared with your loved one who died. Why not make those special meals part of your remembering in the future?

DAY 96
CURIOUS

You are as close to God as you choose to be.
—Rick Warren

What happens to us after we die? There are plenty of differing worldviews about that. Some people are curious about a soul's journey to a different realm. Some people wonder if they'll join their loved one in that realm. What about their body? What about their soul? Do they come back and visit?

Examining this in your grief journey might be important. There is almost always a spiritual reaction to grief—the mystery of the afterlife is intriguing for many.

It's okay to wonder and dig a little deeper. It may give you some peace.

DAY 97
BLUE

*How lucky I am to have something that
makes saying goodbye so hard.*
–Winnie the Pooh

BLUE—THE COLOUR WE associate with sadness and grief and a normal reaction to loss. It would be pretty weird if you weren't blue.

Just as there are many colours in life—*blue* can change. You might feel like there is only a *sea of blue* surrounding you right now, but as you live life, the feelings inside will change color. That doesn't that mean you won't continue to feel blue from time to time, but the *colors of joy* will return, and the blue will subside.

Hang in there—there's a whole rainbow of life out there for you.

DAY 98
WISH

We ourselves feel that what we are doing is just a drop in the ocean. But the ocean would be less because of that missing drop.
—Mother Teresa

There's an interesting thing about making a wish. We don't usually believe they'll come true. They're just words we say as we blow out candles on a birthday cake or snap the wish bone of a turkey: "Make a wish!" we say.

Sometimes we wish that our loved one had not died. We wish they would come through the front door again. We know it's not possible. It's *wishful* thinking.

But let's turn it around: "What is your loved one wishing for *you* in your future?" They may have a realistic wish for you that will come true. After all, they know you best.

DAY 99
TOGETHER

The need for connection and community is primal, as fundamental as the need for air, water, and food.
—Dean Ornish

WE NEED PEOPLE in our lives, especially when we are grieving. Social isolation can lead to all kinds of unhealthy outcomes.

The need for others is especially pronounced when we are grieving. Certainly, we need our *alone time* to think and reflect upon what we miss—the person who died. But we are also built for community.

Whether we choose to spend time with one other person or more than one (depending upon personality), we need to be together. It's the healthy choice.

DAY 100
ATTENTION

Listen, I tell you a mystery: We will not all sleep, but we will all be changed — in a flash, in the twinkling of an eye, at the last trumpet. For the trumpet will sound, the dead will be raised imperishable, and we will be changed.
–Paul the Apostle

I LEFT THE ZUCCHINI in our garden and it grew—a lot! I'm not sure what would have happened had I left it any longer. I had forgotten to check up on our vegetable garden and things had grown out of control.

Neither can you leave your grief alone, unattended, without it experiencing some kind of "growth spurt." Ignoring the pain of grief or trying to dull it will only feed it and cause it to grow. Unattended grief will only squeeze out sideways and do things you don't want it to do.

Grief needs your time and attention.

You can engage your grief. If you tend to it intentionally, it can move you in a direction that is helpful and healthful.

DAY 101
HURT

Daring to set boundaries is having the courage to love ourselves even when we risk disappointing others.
—Brené Brown

Is there hurt in your family because of circumstances surrounding the death of your love one? I would urge you not to let it separate you. Your loved one would be sad about that.

It takes a courageous person to return to broken or shattered relationships and forgive. You may say that it's too late, and maybe for now, it is. But perhaps in the future it can be resolved.

Maybe you need to have a solid boundary with someone right now if that relationship is too difficult—and that's wise.

There may be reconciliation in the future.

DAY 102
CONNECTIONS

It's so much darker when a light goes out than it would have been if it had never shone.
–John Steinbeck

I missed four consecutive connections from Washington D. C. to Victoria, B. C. It was a long day of waiting and sitting in three different airports to get to my final destination. Close to twenty-two hours of travelling.

Grief is never a smooth, clean flight. There are always unexpected stops along the way. You'll feel hijacked by sadness one day, anger the next and guilt on a different day.

Grief is not your final destination. It's a continuing journey. Grief will lighten but you will always miss that someone. When grief returns, just hang tight and use the time to remember. It will waylay you for a time, but not forever.

DAY 103
UNEXPECTED

In everyone's life, at some time, our inner fire goes out. It is then burst into flame by an encounter with another human being. We should all be thankful for those people who rekindle the inner spirit.
—Albert Schweitzer

Are there surprises in your grief journey? What a crazy question—of course there are!

You can't plan your reactions to grief. They just come. There are many changes taking place in your life—probably more than you ever anticipated.

Every change requires a response. That's just what transition is. It can be overwhelming.

What about managing what you can and asking for help for the rest?

A friend can lighten the load—if you are willing to reach out.

So often people want to help but wonder how best to do that. You may have to let them know what you need.

DAY 104
ANNIVERSARY

Death is no more than passing from one room into another. But there's a difference for me, you know. Because in that other room I shall be able to see.
—Helen Keller

It comes every year.

The anniversary of a death.

And it reminds you of the person whom you will always miss.

The closer that anniversary comes, the more anxious or sad you feel. It brings back that pang of loss.

You wish you could just bypass it—jump over that date.

But what about honoring that day instead?

Spend time planning for it. Ask yourself how you might honor your loved one by giving them a place in your day.

DAY 105
CURIOUS QUESTION #5

Is there something you would like to say to *Suffering* when it overwhelms you?

THE GRIEF JOURNEY can be described as *Suffering*, which is anything to do with pain. When you miss someone special, you experience pain.

You wonder how long this suffering will last when grief seems too hard to manage. Unfortunately, there is no escape from the emotional pain of grief. However, you can address *Suffering*—as you would a person—and ask it to lighten up so that you can find joy in your day.

Is there something you would like to say to *Suffering* right now that would give you some respite from the pain of grief that you are experiencing?

DAY 106
TURTLE

The whole point of getting things done is knowing what to leave undone.
—Oswald Chambers

You've heard it said, "Slow and steady wins the race." But maybe you haven't heard it applied to the grief journey.

Time doesn't actually heal grief, but intentional movement does.

You will heal once you move into your grief, experience the pain of missing and consider thoughtfully what life will give you in your next chapter.

Be a turtle, not a rabbit. Move slowly—but move.

DAY 107
TRICYCLE

I should know enough about loss to realize that you never really stop missing someone—you just learn to live around the huge gaping hole of their absence.
—Alyson Noel, Evermore

WE BOUGHT A tricycle for one of our grandsons. It was his first *trike*. He needed three wheels before he was comfortable riding on two.

It's no different in grief. At the outset, you need that extra support in your life. Those friends give you confidence and maybe even push you a little. It may be uncomfortable initially. It takes a little practice before you find your balance. A little push and then, all of a sudden, everything *clicks* and you're on your way.

Then you venture out—on your own—and figure out what is next for you.

DAY 108
UNDERSTANDING

The same thing happened today that happened yesterday, only to different people.
–Walter Winchell

YOUR GRIEF STORY is very different from the person's next you.

Sure, there may be some similarities, but there are so many factors that make it different. That's because you are uniquely you. Your story is not identical to anyone else's.

Be careful when others say they "totally understand" what you are going through because they've "been there."

Sure, learn from others but don't assume your journey will be the same.

You will discover what works for you. It may take effort. It may be messy. But you'll come out ahead in the end.

DAY 109
FEAR

The reality is that you will grieve forever. You will not get over the loss of a loved one; you'll learn to live with it. You will heal and you will rebuild yourself around the loss you have suffered. You will be whole again, but you will never be the same. Nor should you be the same nor would you want to.
—Elisabeth Kübler-Ross

We fear the unknown.

Never having been in a particular situation before, we're afraid of what's up ahead. We have no idea—or at least only a vague idea—what might happen. That's a tough place to be.

There is a very real lack of control in grief. For some, that's exhausting, stressful, unnerving.

What lies ahead for me?
Will I be okay?
What will my life be like now?
…all normal questions.

But can you sit in the unknown for a moment?

Don't try to figure everything out at once. Do what you need to do but give some space between you and your future.

DAY 110
SHORE

Some bright morning when this life is over, I'll fly away.
–Allison Krauss and Gillian Welch, I'll Fly Away

There are many shores that we land on in our lives. Have you ever set out on a journey not knowing where you might end up? We usually plan when we're taking a trip somewhere.

In grief, there's no map and no final destination. There's just another journey. You'll always miss that person.

The journey of living continues—shore to shore. Why not take the person who has died into your boat and travel together?

DAY 111
REACTIONS

Knowledge is of more value than gold.
  –King Solomon

We have many reactions to grief.

They are like the lights on our car's dashboard, telling us that something needs to be looked at under the hood.

A reaction has to do with what is happening to us—it's an automatic reflex from within. It's inadvertent, occurs quickly and often comes without warning. We don't have too much control over reactions. They well up from within us because we're missing someone who was an important part of our lives.

Reactions are clear indicators that something is going on that needs our attention. Reactions indicate that something that wasn't our choice is still impacting us in a big way.

We need to bring these reactions into the open, call them out, take account of them and ask deeper questions about them.

DAY 112
HAPPY

I just ate six happy meals, and I am still depressed.
—Ziggy

Y̲OU'RE NOT HAPPY right now.
In fact, even the concept of *happiness* upsets you. Fair enough.

Someone has died and you miss them—very much.

But if you do have a *happy* day in the midst of some sad days, don't feel guilty about it.

Something or someone might just bring some joy to your life when you need it the most. It doesn't take away from the love you have for the person who died—grief and love are two sides of the same coin.

But be open to these spurts of happiness that bring beauty to your day.

DAY 113
UNPREDICTABLE

Today I give myself permission to miss them.
—Unknown

Life is unpredictable and the unknown, difficult to manage. We feel we have very little control over the future, especially if we have experienced multiple losses.

Try to focus on what *is* known and what you *can* control.

When fearful thoughts of the unknown start to build in your mind say, "Not today, I've got enough to manage right now. Thanks, but no thanks."

DAY 114
HEAVY

*God grant me the serenity to accept the things
I cannot change, courage to change the things I
can and the wisdom to know the difference.*
—Reinhold Niebuhr

GRIEF IS HEAVY when you're carrying the full weight of it all at once. Is there something you can let go of that is dragging you down?

Why not make a list of everything you are dealing with right now? Write everything down that comes to mind.

Now, what is the top priority on that list? What can you do today? What can wait until tomorrow?

There's a weird dichotomy in grief—we either try to do everything at once and get overwhelmed or freeze and do nothing.

If there are too many items on our to-do list, we don't know where to start. Then we wait and get frustrated that we aren't accomplishing anything.

Don't push yourself. Lighten your load by doing only one or two tasks a day. That's more than enough.

DAY 115
EXIT

She was no longer wrestling with grief but could sit down with it as a lasting companion and make it a sharer in her thought.
—George Eliot

The sign said, "EXIT," in big, red letters—the way out, in case of emergency.

Don't you wish you had an emergency exit for your grief? Your heart is torn because you miss your loved one and it feels like an emergency. Your entire being wants to flee.

The truth is, you experience the pain of grief because you *miss* and you *love*.

When the pain seems like too much, ask someone who is important to you to be with you for a while. You can't exit your pain; you have to sit with it and experience it. But sometimes it's worth inviting someone into your space to be near you.

DAY 116
CREAM

You can go your whole life collecting days, and none will outweigh the one you wish you had back.
–Mitch Albom

CREAM RISES TO the top even though it's heavier than the whey below it.

What's heaviest in your grief journey right now? What's rising to the top of the heap? Maybe it's a practical concern, maybe emotional, perhaps it's uncertainty about the future or how to manage the people around you. Regardless it's overwhelming and weighing you down.

Why not make a list of all that is on your mind (and heart)? Decide to focus on the heaviest thing first and take action to lighten your load. You can't do it all, but you can do one thing.

That's more than enough for today.

DAY 117
DOUBLE-DOUBLE

There is no grief like the grief that does not speak.
–Henry Wadsworth Longfellow

Tim Horton's is an iconic chain of coffee shops in Canada. The term "double-double"—meaning two cream, two sugar—is a phrase they coined and is common jargon for anyone ordering a coffee north of the 49th parallel. "I'll have a large double-double, please." You don't even have to use the word *coffee*. The server will know what you mean—even if you're not at Tim Horton's when you order it!

What's the most common phrase you hear in your grief journey spoken by people around you? Are they words that make you feel like you're understood? The right word spoken to you at the right time can make your day.

But some of the common platitudes might not be so helpful.

Be bold and let people know what words are helpful to you and which words you prefer not to hear. People don't always know. But you do!

DAY 118
DISAPPOINTMENT

Few things in the world are more powerful than a positive push. A smile. A world of optimism and hope. A "you can do it" when things are tough.
—Richard M. DeVos

Disappointment. It's part of life. It's part of grief too.

Someone you thought would be there for you in your loss hasn't been available. Perhaps you even feel ignored or distanced—emotionally or geographically. Regardless why they're absent, it's difficult to manage the emotions that result from disappointment with people whom you had counted on but weren't there for you.

Many people are uncomfortable with loss and don't know what to do or how to respond to those who are grieving.

So, spend more time with those who *have* shown up in your life. They care and are comfortable with your loss.

DAY 119
UNPLEASANT

*There was never a night or a problem
that could defeat sunrise or hope.*
—Bernard Williams

There is pain in grief as well as unpleasant surprises that are difficult to manage.

But sometimes there are unexpected surprises that bring joy, even in the midst of unpleasantness. These surprises give you hope even if the future might feel uncertain. Hang onto those moments—they're telling you something. What do they say?

"You're going to be okay."

DAY 120
MOON

To live in hearts, we leave behind is not to die.
–Thomas Campbell

I LOVE HEARING THESE words from my grandkids: "I love you to the moon and back."

That's a lot of love.

It's interesting that love for a person explodes when they are no longer physically present in our lives.

We have always loved them, but when we miss them, the emotional expression of love and the need to be connected again are so strong.

Love does not end when a person dies. It just can't be expressed the same way as it was before.

But you can still say, "I love you to the moon and back." Your love is legit—it doesn't die with the person.

DAY 121
MORE

No man ever steps in the same river twice, for it is not the same river and he is not the same man.
—Heraclitus

Any type of loss results in *more*.

More of what?

More loss.

When someone dies, you experience the loss not only of that person but also all the *mini losses* that come as a result of that person no longer being part of your life. Little things you didn't even think about when they were alive.

These multiple losses can impact how you transition through grief. Sometimes you don't even recognize these compounded losses—they can be really subtle. It means that you have to go easy on yourself. Cut yourself some slack.

DAY 122
OPEN

The weird, weird thing about devastating loss is that life actually goes on. When you're faced with a tragedy, a loss so huge that you have no idea how you can live through it, somehow, the world keeps turning, the seconds keep ticking.
–James Patterson

THE PICKLE JAR was hard to open. Really hard. We all gave it a shot, but the lid was on tight.

We tapped the side, put it under hot water. One person held the jar with two hands, and another tried to twist off the lid. Nothing seemed to work—and we really wanted those pickles for the sandwiches we were making.

I knew we just needed to break the seal—a little air was all we'd need. I was bound and determined to succeed. I decided to soak it in some hot water. Ten minutes later, I gently tapped the sides and the top of the lid and finally it released. Success!

Don't work too hard at grief. Just work on it enough to release some of the pressure when it gets to be too much.

DAY 123
ALWAYS

*Good morning, Sun! Each day I'm always
a bit relieved that you have decided to come
back again… and give us another chance*
−Ziggy

I LIKE WILLIE NELSON's tune, *Always on My Mind*. The title says it all. That's a common theme for anyone at the beginning of their grief journey—the person we miss is always on our mind.

It's true that when someone dies, they are on our mind continually—even more so than when they were alive.

Why is that?

We are adapting to a new reality without this person. Our mind just won't let go. The relationship was just too important.

That's how the mind works. It needs to adjust. In time, the brain with its capacity for memory will give that person a place forever but also create space for everything else that is important in life.

DAY 124
RIPPLE

*A beautiful, colorful rainbow could not exist
if it were not for the rain of a grey day—
it was born from the very droplets of it.*
−Unknown

THE DEATH OF someone dear to you can cause a ripple effect of other losses, many of which may require your immediate attention.

Sometimes these secondary losses take your time and energy initially. They may be practical issues that you need to manage in the mist of grief and transition: finances, occupation, moving, paperwork, family members, etc.

I have often heard people say, "I haven't had time to grieve because of all this other stuff that I need to deal with!"

One loss at time. In the midst of *all this other stuff* you are still missing someone special. Don't feel guilty about trying to adapt to life. Don't be hard on yourself. You are doing your best.

DAY 125
RING

The tongue has the power of life and death.
—King Solomon

You wish the phone would ring. Mostly you just wish the voice on the other end was the person you miss. What a gift it would be to hear their voice one more time. If they could phone you, what would they say to you to comfort your heart today?

It's not the same, I know, but because you had a relationship with this person, and shared life and conversation, you probably have a pretty good idea what their words to you might be.

You could even say out loud, "Thank you for those words. They really helped me."

DAY 126
CURIOUS QUESTION #6

What is *Quietness* telling you right now?

QUIETNESS CAN FEEL like a curse if it doesn't include thoughtful reflection.

Quietness can also be a gift in the midst of mayhem. It offers you the opportunity to remain still—no movement. Just a deep breath.

If in *Quietness* negative thoughts and obsessive emotions cling to you, you may need to address them. Tell them to leave the space that you and *Quietness* created together for personal reflection.

Speak and they will listen.

DAY 127
TRUE

An eternal memory... until we meet again: Those special memories will always bring a smile if only I could have you back for just a little while. Then we could sit and talk again just like we used to do, you always meant so very much and always will do too. The fact that you're no longer here will always cause me pain, but you're forever in my heart until we meet again.

—Unknown

Fear often tells us stories that aren't true, making us frightened of the future.

We may not know what our future holds, but we do know who loves us—and that might just be enough to help us take small steps forward.

DAY 128
WELCOME

*Each person's grief journey is as unique
as a fingerprint or a snowflake.*
—EARL GROLLMAN

"Welcome, visitor. How long do you plan to stay? I've known you before, but you are different this time around. What's your name?"

"Grief."

"Yes, we have met before. And I suppose I must get to know you again."

DAY 129
CYCLES

*Grief and love are conjoined—you
don't get one without the other.*
—Jandy Nelson

You probably don't want to hear that grief will cycle back into your life, but it will—especially at the outset of your loss. When it does, it may come in the back door and surprise you. Some people refer to this as a *grief burst*.

When you experience a grief burst, there are a couple of things that can happen: you feel the sadness of missing, but if you sit in that emotion, it can be turned into an opportunity to honor the memory of your loved one as a gift. The grief that is returning is a sign that you loved someone deeply and always will.

When grief cycles back, it just means you miss that person and had something beautiful with them.

DAY 130
POTTER

Grief is a process, not a state.
–Anne Grant

I LOVE WATCHING A potter work the clay. It's amazing how earth and water come together to form something useful and artistic.

Getting your hands into grief means that you have the opportunity to shape and mold something. If you aren't intentional with it, it will remain an unseemly lump. Working with your grief affords you the chance to create something new.

There will be events in your grief journey that are beyond your control, to be sure. But the things you can control—where you can be hands-on—allow you to begin to work and create a new and different you.

In some ways, you are now different because your loved one has died, but you are still you—and can do some honing as a potter shapes clay.

DAY 131
HOT CHOCOLATE

Sorrow is so easy to express and yet so hard to tell.
–Joni Mitchell

It was a cold day. We had finished working hard—some did the farm chores while others checked to see if more baby calves had been born. I shoveled off the skating rink. It was -30 Celsius. With frozen cheeks and tingling toes, we came back into the house in the late afternoon. Naturally, it was time for…hot chocolate!

As we sat around the table together, I couldn't help but give thanks for each person. There is something beautiful about sharing life with others.

I wonder if this is an important part of your grief—sitting around the table together and giving thanks for each person who is in your life right now.

DAY 132
HEARING

Words kill, words give life; they're either poison or fruit—you choose.
—King Solomon

WHEN THERE ARE so many voices speaking into your grief walk, it's difficult to decide what voice you need to hear and what is most helpful. Sometimes you just want to put in ear plugs in when you've heard enough opinions.

When we say that someone has *selective hearing,* we usually mean it in a less-than-favourable way. But in grief, selective hearing can be an asset. Closing our ears to the world is necessary when we feel overwhelmed with too much information. You can choose what words you want to hear and receive.

DAY 133
GAP

It takes strength to make your way through grief, to grab hold of life and let it pull you forward.
—Patti Davis

"Mind the gap!" the automated message says every time the subway doors close in the London Underground. They've said that since 1968.

The gap between the start of our grief journey and our *new* life without the person who has died can feel like a chasm. While we can't put a timeframe on grief, there seems to be a period (that can vary) in which deep wrestling takes place as we come to grips with our new identity. The question we ask—consciously or unconsciously—is often, "Who am I now without this person physically present in my life?"

DAY 134
PITCH

What we have once enjoyed deeply we can never lose. All that we love deeply becomes a part of us.
–Helen Keller

"You're a little flat," she said to me as I tried to sing. Some people have perfect pitch—you can ask them for a note, and they'll pull it out of thin air. Others, like me, need some help to find their starting note.

Where do you even start in your grief journey? Probably off-key and out of tune–that's perfectly normal. There is disharmony in your life. The one you used to *sing life* with has died. The song has changed. And for the moment, you may not even feel like singing at all.

DAY 135
COASTER

Come back. Even as a shadow, even as a dream.
—Euripides

It's the coaster on which he set his cup of coffee every morning. It's not worth much but it means everything to me because it reminds me of him. I can see him in his chair and picture his face. I watch him turn the pages of the paper and see his smile.

I wait for his voice, "We should have some breakfast." He smiles and gets up, moving towards the table.

What's something you keep that connects you with the person you are missing?

Why not find that item and take time to remember that special person in your life?

DAY 136
PHOTOS

The pain passes, but the beauty remains.
—Pierre Auguste Renoir

"Hey, Dad, do you have some of the old photo albums I could borrow," my eldest son, Devon, asked.

I found it an interesting request—especially the timing. Then I understood.

He wanted to introduce his new girlfriend (now his wife) to his mom who had died at age forty-seven.

The best way for him to do that was to share photos and stories of her.

For Devon, photos were the means of bringing his mom into his world for a few moments.

DAY 137
QR

*In my dream, I was drowning my sorrows
but my sorrows they'd learned to swim.*
–U2, Until the End of the World

WE ALL SEEM to be getting more comfortable scanning QR codes—they're everywhere. If you have a smart phone and you point it at the encrypted code, it takes you directly to where it wants you to go.

Do you wish you could just "QR" your loved one whom you're missing? Just for a moment, you wish you could be in their presence, give them a hug or hear their voice.

But you can "QR" them, in a way, by giving thanks for what you *did* have and for the time that you *did* experience with them. It takes you to them.

What are the things you're most thankful for that bring you back to your loved one?

DAY 138
LANGUAGE

*Honest listening is one of the best medicines
we can offer the dying and the bereaved.*
—Jean Cameron

CARELESS WORDS CAN really have a negative impact on people who are grieving. Comments that are thoughtless—even well-meaning—can send them into a tailspin.

If you hear someone speaking words to a grieving person and you know their comments will be hurtful rather than helpful, please don't be afraid to step in and say something.

And if you yourself hear words from others that are not helping, gently let people know that you would prefer they not comment.

It's always better to be truthful with others. Some people just don't know what to say that is helpful and may need a little guidance.

DAY 139
MINUTES

*Walk on, walk on with hope in your
heart and you'll never walk alone.*
—Rodgers and Hammerstein, Carousel

I missed out. Time just slipped away so quickly. Now they're gone and I regret every time that I didn't say "yes" to spending time with my loved one.

But would there ever have been enough time with this person?

Life is a series of moments shared in time and space—these minutes are so important.

Instead of focusing on the time you missed with this person who's gone, turn towards the moments you had that were meaningful.

DAY 140
GRAFTING

Never let the fear of striking out get in your way.
—Babe Ruth

Many people describe grief as feeling "cut off" from their loved one. "I feel like a part of me is gone forever," is a phrase that I often hear from people.

Don't let "gone forever" become part of your relationship with the person whom you love.

Why not graft this person into your life?

Consider yourself as a tree with many branches and leafy offshoots. Each branch represents a person. Each leaf is a characteristic, value, principle or learning that you can ascribe to a person who has influenced or impacted your life.

What part of this person will you take with you in your life as you move forward?

DAY 141
SLIPPERS

Love dies only when growth stops.
—Pearl S. Buck

My mother-in-law gave some slippers to my wife, Erica, a few months ago and they fit her perfectly. Mom didn't need them anymore.

Then Mom died in October.

We honored her at her funeral.

When we returned home, there, sitting on the stool in our room, were the slippers she had given Erica. For a moment as I looked at them, they seemed to come alive. I could hear Mom's infectious laugh, see her broad smile and feel her warm hugs again.

It brought me closer to her for those few moments and it felt good. I love her so much and miss her deeply.

I have a few other items that remind me of Mom. I'm going to hold them close to my heart until that time that we meet again.

DAY 142
MEATBALLS

Her absence is like the sky, spread over everything.
–C. S. Lewis, A Grief Observed

I WAS MAKING MEATBALLS and invited the grandkids to help me. It took a little longer than I had anticipated, but that was okay. We got our hands mucky together as each of us rolled out the meatballs in varying sizes and shapes. Some didn't look too much like meatballs—but that was fine too.

Grief looks different for everyone. It comes in all sizes and shapes, experienced uniquely by each person. No such thing as "one-size-fits-all" in grief.

Grief may be unique, but what is shared is missing the person. Sharing this experience together—and not alone—will help you in our grief journey.

DAY 143
TURBULENCE

*There is a time to weep and a time to laugh;
a time to mourn and a time to dance.*
—King Solomon

"Please return to your seat and secure your seat belt," the flight attendant said over the public-address system. "The captain has turned on the seat belt sign. We will be going through some turbulence," he continued.

As passengers, we couldn't see the turbulence ahead, but thankfully, because of the weather radar display in the cockpit, the pilot could predict the rough ride ahead.

No one can deny that grief is a rough ride—even if we can't predict how it will affect us. But we know it's there and that it can be turbulent.

So, when grief comes, put on your seat belt and know that you will need to absorb some bumps. Also know that eventually the turbulence will pass, and you will be able to get out of your seat and walk around again.

There will be another flight!

DAY 144
REMEMBERING

When someone you love dies, and you're not expecting it, you don't lose her all at once; you lose her in pieces over a long time—the way the mail stops coming, and her scent fades from the pillows and even from the clothes in her closet and drawers. Gradually, you accumulate the parts of her that are gone. Just when the day comes—when there's a particular missing part that overwhelms you with the feeling that she's gone, forever—there comes another day, and another specifically missing part.

–John Irving

Sometimes you wonder if others have forgotten about your loved one who has died and feel alone in your remembering of them.

Having someone else acknowledge that they are missing this person as well can lift the cloak of loneliness you feel.

Hearing a story about what they miss is a comforting experience in the midst of sadness.

And you find yourself thanking that person for remembering with you.

DAY 145
BLANKET

Without you in my arms, I feel an emptiness in my soul. I find myself searching the crowds for your face—I know it's an impossibility, but I cannot help myself.
—Nicholas Sparks

I HAVE A FAVOURITE blanket that I wrap myself in when I watch TV. I hunt for it when it goes missing or gets put away.

When a loved one dies, we long to be wrapped in their love once again. We look for healthy ways to feel their presence around us.

How about wrapping yourself in your favourite blanket and thinking about how much you were loved by this person and how much you loved them?

DAY 146
RECIPE

To me, my recipes are priceless
—Colonel Sanders

My wife just finished making stuffing for the turkey. The recipe has been passed down from my father who died many years ago. We still use it for every one of our turkey dinners.

We know exactly what ingredients to include. We don't add or take away anything so that we can enjoy the same flavor each time we taste it and remember Dad.

I wish there were recipe we could follow for grief. It would make it so much easier. But there isn't. So, you'll need to work it out, adding the ingredients that are most helpful to you.

DAY 147
DAY

The song is ended but the melody lingers on.
—IRVING BERLIN

"ONE DAY AT a time." We hear it all the time. There's a lot of truth to that old adage though. We wonder how we'll make it through the day without feeling lonely or sad. Truthfully? We won't.

It's a heartache. A big one.

You can't fill the space in your heart that belonged to your loved one—that space is theirs and no one else's. The love you shared, the time you spent, the relationship you had with that person was significant and deserves to have a place in your heart forever.

But that doesn't mean that you can't create new spaces in your heart.

DAY 148
CURIOUS QUESTION #7

What is *Sadness* telling you about your life?

SADNESS HAS A story. It always does.

Sadness reminds you how important your loved one was to you and how much you miss them. For that reason, *Sadness* can be a friend—but you probably wonder how long its intensity will last.

Is there something in your life right now that *Sadness* can't touch—something that brings you a measure of relief? *Sadness* isn't all there is.

How might you balance it out?

DAY 149
FOCUS

Love is like standing in wet cement, the longer you stay the harder to leave and you can never leave without leaving your marks behind.
—UNKNOWN

IT'S HARD TO focus when you are grieving. You have things to do but your mind is preoccupied. Distracting thoughts take up *mental real estate*.

What do I mean by that? Matters of the past. Concerns about the future. How much time do you spend in those two zones? If you took stock of your thoughts, you'd probably find that most of your mental energy goes toward revisiting the past or worrying about the future.

We constantly hear the mantra: *Live in the present.* That's challenging when the present forces us to press into our grief. But that's where real living takes place. You don't want to miss out on what you have to offer others—right here, right now.

Take notice of today and see what happens.

DAY 150
CARERFUL

Most psychiatrists agree that sitting in a pumpkin patch is an excellent therapy for a troubled mind.
—Linus Van Pelt, Peanuts

One of the signs that we're struggling in our grief is if we engage in unhelpful or even risky behavior.

We need to be careful in our grief journey. Escalating emotions can (if we're not careful) lead to unhealthy choices that are both new and potentially detrimental to ourselves and others.

As difficult as it might be, it would be a good idea to check in with a friend or family member once in a while and ask this simple question: "Is there anything you have noticed in my behavior that concerns you?"

This is being vulnerable and accountable.

And it will save you a lot of heartache in the future.

DAY 151
BATTERY

Fun is good.
—Dr. Seuss

Low battery. It's a warning to plug in your device. Are you feeling low on energy? You might consider recharging your battery with these things:

- Eating well
- Getting plenty of rest
- Giving back
- Getting exercise
- Playing again

All these will be of benefit to you by reducing your stress by lowering your cortisol levels and increasing positive hormones that are lacking in your body.

DAY 152
FRUSTRATION

Sometimes I lie awake at night and ask, "Where have I gone wrong?" Then a voice says to me, "This is going to take more than one night."
–Charles Schulz

WHEN WE FEEL as though life is out of control, we get frustrated—with ourselves, with others and with life in general.

Sometimes changing the environment helps to reduce that sense of anxiety.

Go for a walk. Leave the house. Take a short holiday. Go out for supper with a friend.

Choosing a different environment takes you out of a situation that is choking you.

Take a break and get away.

DAY 153
SOUNDS

Music exalts each joy, allays each grief,
expels diseases, softens every pain.
—John Armstrong

Sounds immediately connect us with an important event.

You know this, because when you hear a piece of music, a loon call, a child's laughter, a siren—it can bring you back to an event, experience or person with whom the sound is associated.

You are driving down the road in your car and a song begins to play on the radio. Suddenly you are transported to another time and place. You're with someone you love and feeling like you did when you were a teenager.

Or you're on a lake and you hear the haunting call of a loon. You can practically taste the morning coffee you had with your loved one at the cabin every summer.

Sometimes it's a sad memory, sometimes it's a happy one.

Don't be surprised when a sound brings the memory of a friend or loved one back to you.

DAY 154
FOOTPRINTS

When you are sorrowful look again in your heart, and you shall see that in truth you are weeping for that which has been your delight.
—Kahlil Gibran

The tide was out, so we walked out toward the ocean on the smooth, packed sand—our footprints visible behind us for quite a distance.

Soon the tide began to rise. We turned around and headed toward shore—we couldn't help but notice that our footprints were covered over by the water, never to be seen again.

I believe that people leave indelible footprints in our hearts. Even though the person is no longer physically present in life, they have left something with us.

We can invite them to walk with us from time to time and be reminded of what they gave us in life, now a footprint in our grief.

DAY 155
TIMELY

Deep grief sometimes is almost like a specific location, a coordinate on a map of time. When you are standing in that forest of sorrow, you cannot imagine that you could ever find your way to a better place. But if someone can assure you that they themselves have stood in that same place, and now have moved on, sometimes this will bring hope.
—Elizabeth Gilbert

Some people have a knack for saying the right thing at the right time.

"I really needed to hear that."

Who has been important in your grief journey? Who has spoken wisdom and discernment into your life?

Keep them close to you.

DAY 156
SHADE

Plans?... I suppose I'll sleep a little this morning. Then this afternoon, I'll take a short nap and later on, I'll try to get some more sleep. Those are good plans!
—Snoopy, Peanuts

IT'S WAY TOO hot! I need to get into the shade!
In a desert, it's near impossible to find shade.
Grief often feels like a shade-less wasteland. How *do* you cool off?
Where do *you* go to find shade?

DAY 157
GARBAGE

The irony of grief is that the person you most want to talk to about it is no longer here.
–Unknown

"Garbage in and garbage out." No doubt you've heard that phrase many times. It's even more important in a grief journey. What you read, hear and view is important to discern when you are grieving. Everyone has a different angle or perspective depending upon their personal experience, training, discipline or worldview. Grief is deep and wide, just like all the advice people will try to give you.

But this is your story to write. It will be important to focus on a few trusted sources when seeking out wisdom on how to *do* grief well. Throw the rest in the garbage—you'll be thankful you did.

DAY 158
RESEARCH

Sometimes, when I see my granddaughters make small discoveries of their own, I wish I were a child.
—Dr. Seuss

There are so many who claim to know the truth and the way through grief. The stages of grief are replaced with numerous methods, often researched and made popular as *the next best thing*.

Certainly, science as a discipline examines very interesting aspects of grief and draws conclusions for consideration. But don't hang your hat on science—there will always be another *hat* to try on sooner than later.

Consider interesting aspects of research but don't let research be your compass through grief.

DAY 159
PROMISE

*So, it's true, when all is said and done,
grief is the price we pay for love.*
—E. A. Bucchianeri

WHEN WE MAKE and keep a promise, we show our loyalty to another person. It's a commitment: "I will do this, no matter what it takes. I will hold up my end of the bargain."

When someone has died, we hear words of promise that come back to us: "Promise me you'll go on." "Promise me that you'll take care of our children." "Promise me that you won't sell the house." We often agree because we don't want to upset the person who is dying.

Promises like these can actually hold us back though. The only promise that we *can* keep and be true to is our love for that person. We can always love even though it may be different than before.

DAY 160
GOODNIGHT

*To bring anything into your life,
imagine that it's already there.*
—Richard Bach

"GOODNIGHT" FEELS APPROPRIATE when you know you are going to wake up and say, "Good morning!" to your loved one.

But falling asleep at night is really tough if you know that the next morning your loved one won't be there because they've died.

Each day that you wake up is a reminder the person is no longer there. Your heart hurts and the day hasn't even started yet. You think, "How am I going to make it? It would have been easier if I'd just stayed asleep."

That may be true, except that once you experience the reality of loss, you're better able to mourn this person.

It's so tough—this person is not coming back. Now you will have to decide the best way to remember them in the future.

DAY 161
ENDURING

*When someone you love becomes a memory,
the memory becomes a treasure.*
—Unknown

How do you establish an enduring connection with the person whom you still love?

That might seem like an odd question to you.

Do you love this person? Of course, you do.

Will you always love this person? Absolutely.

If you don't spend time with a person in this life, you will grow apart. It's actually no different from a person who has died.

I'm not saying that you should make the person who died an idol in your life. That's unhealthy.

It's really about honouring the relationship you had with your loved one. You do that by maintaining an enduring connection.

How will you include them in your life and next chapter?

DAY 162
DYNAMICS

There are three needs of the griever: To find the words for the loss, to say the words aloud and to know that the words have been heard.
—Victoria Alexander

YOUR RELATIONSHIPS WILL likely change when someone close to you dies. This can even happen within families.

You may be surprised by this. People you thought were rock-solid are now responding in ways that are impacting you and the rest of the family in negative ways.

Family dynamics are challenging because there are so many different personalities that make up your *tribe*. People's personality traits or behaviour is often exacerbated in grief.

Setting some boundaries with people may be necessary for a time if you are being negatively impacted by them—even (and maybe especially) if it's a family member.

DAY 163
SPIRITUAL

He will wipe every tear from their eyes. There will be no more death or mourning or crying or pain, for the old order of things has passed away.
—BOOK OF REVELATION 21:4

THE DEATH OF a loved one often sparks spiritual questions about the soul, life after death, reincarnation or even God. Whether openly or privately, I often hear people question God—how they define that differs—but they still reach out to something bigger that's outside themselves.

People's questions seem to fall under two categories. The first category is usually more *general*:

- Where is my loved one?
- Is there an after-life?
- Where does the soul go?
- Will I see them again?
- Can they come back and talk to me?

The second category is usually more *personal*:

- Why did this happen to me?
- Who am I without this person in my life?
- Where is God in all this?
- What does this mean for my future?
- What does this say about the world I live in?

When one experiences intense loss, one cannot help but examine deep things to do with the soul.

DAY 164
FRIENDS

A lot of people have gone further than they thought they could because someone else thought they could.
−Zig Ziglar

YOU WONDER WHY your friend is keeping their distance from you since the death of your loved one?

Try saying this to them: "I miss our friendship and I'm just wondering if we can talk about it. I think we are both missing (person's name). I really need you to be on this journey with me."

See what happens. You don't shoot, you don't score. Maybe your friend is just waiting for you to say something.

DAY 165
LIGHTBULB

The best angle to approach life's challenges is always the try-angle.
–Ziggy

When a lightbulb burns out, timing is everything.

If it burns out during the day—no problem. But if it's in the middle of the night when you are trying to find the washroom in the cabin you just rented, it's a problem.

That happened to me recently. I hugged the wall and gingerly felt my way forward. I was careful to feel each step with my foot as I descended the stairs. I had no recollection of the floor plan. The cabin was new to me. Where was the wall? Would I hit it? If only the lightbulb had not gone out at night. I groped around and made it—just in time.

There is so much stumbling and casting about in grief.

It's difficult to find a way through. But you will. Take your time.

DAY 166
MASK

Life is full of grief, to exactly the degree we allow ourselves to love other people.
—Orson Scott Card, Shadow of the Giant

MOST PEOPLE WHO are grieving mask what they're experiencing in their loss—to others or even to themselves. It's normal. We all walk this personal journey uniquely.

We should consider taking off the *I'm OK* mask and invite human connection. If you ever needed others, it's when you are grieving. Grief is a really tough space to live in—don't go it alone.

We really do need people in our grief walk.

We need to be *seen* by others whom we can trust in our journey.

DAY 167
CULTURE

*We're all human beings, in the end,
despite our differences.*
–Timothy Morton

EVERY CULTURE HAS its unique ways of doing grief. What are the rituals? What are the expectations from others? What do people say to you or about you? What does your culture say about grief and the journey that follows?

Just knowing cultural differences—even though they may not be your own—may help you to discover your unique way of grieving.

DAY 168
DEFLATED

You can't truly heal from a loss until you allow yourself to really feel the loss.
—Mandy Hale

I MUST HAVE HIT the curb with my front tire—it needed some air. A friend pointed it out to me. He said that it looked low. I hadn't noticed prior to him mentioning it.

"You might need to check that out before you drive away," he admonished.

"You're right!" I replied.

"Actually, don't worry…I have a compressor. I'll check it out for you," he said. He checked for nails or leaks and then topped up my tire with air so I could drive home safely.

Have you ever felt deflated in your grief journey?

A good friend can help you out just when you need it most.

DAY 169
CURIOUS QUESTION #8

What legacy about grief do you want to leave to your family?

THIS SEEMS LIKE a strange question, but how you manage, adapt to and speak about grief can impact your family members forever. The words we say and the ways we respond to grief stick in people's minds.

So much of grief is learned from our family of origin. If we have been fortunate to have someone before us model a healthy understanding of grief, then we are blessed.

This might also be the opportune time to break unhealthy grief patterns and create a new model for family members as they observe how you are grieving.

Is it time to leave a *positive grief legacy* behind that will help others in your family for years to come?

How will you embark on your grief journey so that others might learn and benefit in future?

DAY 170
CHOOSE

Dear Valentine, I love you. Whoever you are.
—Charles Schulz

WHAT WILL YOU choose today? Fear or love? Many of our reactions to grief are fear-based. Fear of the unknown. Fear that we won't make it.

Fear disrupts our lives and robs us of joy. Holding on to fear affects not only our emotions—it also impacts the physical make-up of our body and mind.

The opposite of this is love. When a person chooses to love or to be loved, fear is attenuated, and their heart and mind can begin to be open to life-giving possibilities.

Gratitude is a good place to start in eliminating fear. Then love brings light and pushes out the darkness.

DAY 171
MONOPOLY

Well, everyone can master a grief but he that has it.
—WILLIAM SHAKESPEARE

EVERYONE WANTS TO pull the "get out of jail free" card in *Monopoly*. What person doesn't want to be in the game? Even when it's your turn, you have to roll the right number before you can move. You're stuck. Luck needs to be on your side.

"I feel stuck. I'm not moving." I've heard that many times from grievers. Our emotions feel imprisoned by grief as we mourn the loss of attachment to the person who is no longer present. It's not that you're not moving, it's that they have. And that makes it tough to feel like you're *out of jail*.

DAY 172
RECOVER

*Life is 10% what happens to you and
90% how you react to it.*
−Charles R. Swindoll

WHILE I BELIEVE that healing in grief can take place over time, I don't believe we can recover from grieving someone whom we love and are missing.

True, we can't physically bring a person back to us and experience them the way we used to, but we can still love them and bring them into our current narrative. Love can't develop and deepen because it's one-sided now, but love doesn't go away. It's always there—it's just different now.

Don't get caught up in *recovery* language. Grief can last forever because at some level you will always miss. Thinking that somehow you need to *recover* from loving or missing is setting you up for disappointment.

But you will adapt and move forward.

DAY 173
EXPERIENCE

A people without the knowledge of their past history, origin and culture is like a tree without roots
—MARCUS GARVEY

GRIEF IS AN important teacher. All of life's experiences with people are important.

No one likes to experience grief or loss. But it's part of life's journey. We can't run away from it.

Because grief will return, it's important to continue learning from it. It comes back for a reason.

Try to seek the wisdom that comes from a loss experience each time grief visits you.

DAY 174
SERVE

I want you to be concerned about your next-door neighbor. Do you know your next-door neighbor?
—Mother Teresa

HELPING SOMEONE ELSE or volunteering is one of the best ways to reduce stress and fire up the neurochemicals that create empathy and connection.

Isn't it interesting that doing something for someone else also makes us feel good? We tend to believe that when we're drained, downcast or lack motivation due to grief, we should somehow be the recipient of another's service.

Serving is one of the best medicines for ongoing health and happiness—research has shown that over and over.

Try to be of service to someone today and see what happens.

DAY 175
SHORTS

Don't cry because it's over. Smile because it happened.
 –Dr. Seuss

My dad died much too young. I still have his gaudy purple shorts with tropical birds all over them. What 70-year-old man would where shorts like that to go downtown? My father.

Why do I keep them? Do I think that someday I might wear them? Maybe. Maybe not. But for now, they remind of what made my dad unique and why I am so grateful that he was my dad. I love my Dad. I miss my Dad.

DAY 176
SLIDE

Life is so short. I would rather sing one song than interpret the thousand.
—Jack London

"Who's going first?" I shouted. It was a big waterslide on the dock, positioned perfectly to dump any willing swimmer into the fresh mountain lake.

It seems that every family has at least one kid who is a fearless adventurer. In our family, it's Jake, our 7-year-old grandchild. "I'll go!" he shouted as he climbed up the waterslide. We cheered him as he splashed into the water.

We applauded. Other grandkids followed his lead.

So much about grief is in the *starting*. No one wants to embrace a grief journey initially—it's new and we drag our feet.

Choosing to slide into your grief journey intentionally will be so much easier in the long run. And your loved one would be cheering you on, no doubt.

DAY 177
STUFF

Some things cannot be fixed; they can only be carried.
Grief like yours, love like yours, can only be carried.
—Megan Devine

IT'S JUST STUFF. Or is it? Those items that belonged to your loved one and were either important to them or connected you to them are precious. You know deep down that you need to do some sorting, but the timing of that isn't always easy to determine.

Do a little bit at a time—there's no rush. You'll decide in time which objects you keep or hold onto for future remembering.

DAY 178
PICTURES

Only people who are capable of loving strongly can also suffer great sorrow, but this same necessity of loving serves to counteract their grief and heals them.
—Leo Tolstoy

WE HAVE MANY pictures hanging on our walls, fireplace mantels, and in albums. We probably have many more saved to our phones or the iCloud—photos that we pull up whenever we want.

Sometimes it's hard to see a photo of a loved one who has died. Although it can also be heart-warming to see their smiling face, or their goofy expression, or their arm around our shoulder.

I lost some photos on the iCloud. Gone. I couldn't bring them back. It was so disappointing. I've often heard people say, "I can't remember what he/she looks like any longer."

Time to get your photos out and have a day of remembering. I'm certain it will connect you to some very happy memories.

DAY 179
SLICE

You will lose someone you can't live without, and your heart will be badly broken, and the bad news is that you never completely get over the loss of your beloved. But this is also the good news. They live forever in your broken heart that doesn't seal back up. And you come through. It's like having a broken leg that never heals perfectly—that still hurts when the weather gets cold, but you learn to dance with the limp.
—Anne Lamott

GRIEF IS LIKE a pie that needs to be sliced into manageable pieces. Thinking that you can *eat* or *manage* the whole thing at once is "pie in the sky" philosophy.

Adapting to grief takes time and is most effective in thin slices.

Take it slow and easy.

DAY 180
TANGLED

*In the day of prosperity be joyful, but
in the day of adversity consider.*
–King Solomon

Tangled. Confused. Jumbled. Muddled. Do those words describe your thought-life right now? How do you go about choosing to focus on one thing and not another when you are experiencing grief? When you are out-of-sorts, your mind and emotions tend to keep you focused on that which is most troubling or confusing—something that keeps on spinning without a conclusion.

Focussing on something else may give you a rest from that troubling thought and offer you and external perspective—allowing you to look at it from the outside, no longer tangled in its web.

DAY 181
NATURE

A walk in nature walks the soul back home.
−Mary Davis

A friend of mine likes to sit in his backyard and observe his surroundings every morning. He backs onto a creek and a green area and enjoys what is happening around him.

Cup of coffee in his hand, he sits by himself every morning and opens up his ears to the sounds, his eyes to the environment as he drinks it all in.

Walking is another way to take in nature. Research has shown walking to be beneficial when we are feeling discouraged. One 15-minute walk in nature can change your perspective on life.

Nature invites us, hoping to refresh our spirits and speak to us.

DAY 182
NOURISHMENT

Good food warms the heart and feeds the soul.
—A. D. Posey

ONCE IN A while I'm tempted to order French fries. I know they're not good for me, but I really like them. Recently, I have been eating them less frequently. As a result, they are becoming less desirable to me.

We humans are complicated. Comprised of heart, mind, body and soul, we are complex beings.

In grief, we must consider every part of ourselves that requires nourishment and care. When we take care of our whole self, we are better able to navigate the difficult times brought on by grief.

As simplistic as it sounds, what you eat is really important. It can help or hinder how you feel about life.

Following the death of a loved one, it's tempting not to eat well because food takes preparation and perhaps you aren't motivated to put in the effort to cook.

But if you plan ahead and eat meals that are nourishing, you will be glad you did.

DAY 183
CHATTER

Solitude is very different from a time-out from our busy lives. Solitude is the very ground from which community grows. Whenever we pray alone, study, read, write, or simply spend quiet time away from the places where we interact with each other directly, we are potentially opened for a deeper intimacy with each other.

—Henri Nouwen

Background noise is hard to take when it reaches a certain decibel level: Loud chatter in a coffee shop because people have earbuds in while carrying on a conversation with their neighbour; the guy at the table next to you who plays YouTube videos from his phone.

What happened to peace and quiet?

I usually just leave. I don't own the coffee shop.

If it gets to be too much in your grief journey. Too many voices trying to speak into your experience, just leave for a moment.

A little quiet is a good thing. You don't need to listen to every voice.

DAY 184
PEPPER

*All the darkness in the world cannot
extinguish the light of a single candle.*
—Saint Francis of Assisi

PEPPER. WELL ACTUALLY *salt and pepper*. It's natural to say the two together. Take one away and it doesn't seem right. They come as a pair.

You used to be part of a pair, but your other half is gone—no longer there for you. You are so used to that person being by your side.

A relationship doesn't end when a person dies, it just changes. True, you are no longer able to be physically present with this person—at least not in this life—but that doesn't mean the relationship ends.

Memories are strong reminders that the relationship hasn't ended. The stories of you and your loved one are stored in your memory forever.

Even today you can choose to remember their life with you.

DAY 185
NOISE

She was no longer wrestling with the grief but could sit down with it as a lasting companion and make it a sharer in her thoughts.
—George Eliot

GRIEF NEEDS QUIETNESS in order for it to be processed in our hearts and minds.

In a world of information and digital bombardment, we need to be cognisant of the distractions around us and the obstacles that prevent us from going deep.

Grief can be an ally that deepens our human experience—as long as we cut out all the noise that distracts us from engaging our grief.

DAY 186
PATIENCE

Perhaps grief is not about empty, but full. The full breath of life that includes death. The completeness, the cycles, the depth, the richness, the process, the continuity, and the treasure of the moment that is gone the second you are aware of it.
—Alysia Reiner

The sign said to slow down in the construction zone. I did. But he didn't. He sped up and passed me. Gravel flying, I was eating his dust. A couple of minutes later, I saw him again—stopped by a police officer for speeding. I so badly wanted to wave or smile as I drove past him, but refrained from gloating, at least outwardly. Given the dents that he left on my vehicle from loose gravel, I thought I exhibited great restraint and patience.

I'm not always patience but I do know that patience is required in a grief journey. Small changes are more efficacious than big ones. If we rush ahead, we are bound to experience bigger scrapes and dents in our life.

Don't try to pass too quickly through what is happening in your grief experience. Slow down a bit!

DAY 187
SILLY

Humor is mankind's greatest blessing.
—MARK TWAIN

BEING SILLY—IT HELPS with sadness. It's true. If you want to change how you're feeling, why not look at yourself in the mirror and stick out your tongue? Or run through the sprinkler in your yard? Or ride your bike through a muddle puddle? Or have fun playing with young children?

I'll bet you haven't done any of those for a while, let alone when you are grieving and downcast.

Childlike behaviors (as opposed to *childish*) help break up the *adult* in you that needs to discover how to play again.

I challenge you to find the silly in yourself.

DAY 188
ANGEL

Don't be afraid to see what you see.
—RONALD REAGAN

PEOPLE SAY MANY things to sooth themselves or others following the loss of a loved one. Sometimes those things focus on the afterlife. I hear these questions frequently:

- Is my loved one watching over me?
- Has my loved one become a guardian angel to me and my family?
- Does their spirit really return for a visit?
- Do they really send signs to let me know that they're okay?

What do you believe? Have you experienced something mysterious or unusual that has been of encouragement to you? Something that you can't explain but somehow believe was real.

It was for you. Be thankful for that.

DAY 189
DIFFERENT

The pain passes, but the beauty remains.
—Pierre Auguste Renoir

"You HAVE to try this," he said to me. He was pouring molasses on freshly baked bread. "That's *different*," I said apprehensively. "I've never had that before, but I'll try it," I said.

Choosing to step forward into what is new and different following the death of a loved one or friend is really hard. It takes courage. We often think that we are dishonoring the person who has died when we find ourselves feeling joy again.

"I shouldn't be feeling happy," you say to yourself. "The person whom I loved so much is no longer here."

Oddly enough, discovering what is new and different might be the very best way to honor the person who has died. It's a tribute to how they believed in you and loved you.

So, don't give up on something *different* because you haven't experienced it before.

Your loved one who died may be saying to you, "It's okay for you to be happy again."

DAY 190
CURIOUS QUESTION #9

Why is it so difficult to find meaning in life following the death of someone special?

This is a really good question. When someone who is important to us dies, one of our first thoughts (even if we don't verbalize it) is, "Who am I now without this person in my life?" This is really a question about identity. So much of our meaning in life is derived from our relationships. We have meaningful relationships, but then one is snuffed out. Then what?

We make meaning by celebrating what that person brought us and then by being open to how others (in the future) can bring us meaning as well.

Ask yourself, "How did this person bring meaning to my life?" Write down your reflections. Once you see the many ways, you'll begin to give thanks and open yourself to meaning in your next chapter of life as well.

DAY 191
IMPACT

It is not the answer that enlightens, but the question.
—Eugene Lonesco

GRIEF DOES NOT happen in isolation. It impacts the many relationships that are a part of your world.

Grief is a two-way street—as we interact with people, our reactions to grief are influenced by others as well.

Consider the words or actions of those around you (friends, family members or co-workers) and their attempt to engage you in your grief journey. Or not.

Their words or response to you can help or hinder your journey.

People impact the way we do grief. Two ways to mitigate frustration or hurt from those whose intentions may be well-meaning but misguided is to:

1. know that people will impact you and
2. have an answer in place to respond quickly

Sometimes the easiest way to respond to unhelpful comments is to say, "That's a really interesting take on grief. May I share with you my experience of grief?"

Take the lead.

DAY 192
FAVORITE

There are no goodbyes for us. Wherever you are, you will always be in my heart.
—Mahatma Gandhi

I KEPT STUDYING THE menu but couldn't find my favorite meal on it anywhere. How could they just take it away like that? Who decided not to include it on the menu and why?

Have you ever asked why your loved one was taken from you?

You have many people in your life that are important to you, but this one is no longer present, and you wish they were.

Writing this reminded me to cook one of the favorite meals that I used to eat with my dad. As I ate it, I *invited* him to sit with me. It felt good as I remembered him.

DAY 193
PEACE

Deep grief sometimes is almost like a specific location, a coordinate on a map of time. When you are standing in that forest of sorrow, you cannot imagine that you could ever find your way to a better place. But if someone can assure you that they themselves have stood in that same place, and now have moved on, sometimes this will bring hope.
—Elizabeth Gilbert

Is peace accepting the reality that you will no longer have the person who has died in your life?

Or is peace accepting that you will be okay even though you will miss them?

Perhaps it's a little of both.

DAY 194
CALF

Grief is the loudest silence I have ever heard.
—Sally Morgan

"The calf died," my five-year-old grandson told me. "It's in heaven now," he continued.

Jake had a very empathetic tone as he spoke about the calf's demise. I was heartened that my little grandson expressed feelings from a caring heart.

There is nothing more comforting than a person with an empathetic heart when we are grieving—especially when they are able to express their care for us in more than just words.

We don't always need words in our grief journey. We know how important it is when a person comes to us and, without saying a word, touches something within us that feels like love.

DAY 195
FREEDOM

We get no choice. If we love, we grieve.
—Thomas Lynch

Sometimes we want to break the chains of grief and be freed from the hold it has on us. It's heavy and we want it off our back. It's burdensome.

It's interesting that grief is the result of missing someone special. What can drag us down is our struggle to know how to move forward with life without dishonouring the person whom we still love.

DAY 196
BURN

Happiness is anyone and anything that's loved by you.
—Charles Schulz

I F A BURN is bad, we put something on it to soothe it. But what salve can you put on a broken heart?

We hear about heartache—a broken heart—following the death of someone you are close to. It's a real manifestation of grief that has physical ramifications.

Love is a deep emotion linked to experiences of a shared life together—you can't help but have a broken heart when your life is intensely interconnected with someone else's.

Ironically, the salve you need is the very person whom you spent your life with. Now that person is no longer physically present.

But love and gratitude are amazing healing agents for a broken heart.

Try putting those on your heart today and see if they ease the burn of grief.

DAY 197
HELP

Tears shed for another person are not a sign of weakness. They are a sign of a pure heart.
—Jose N. Harris

"I can do it on my own. I don't need any help. I'll be just fine."

"I really don't want to bother anyone with my problems. People are busy."

How often have you heard that from people who are grieving? They don't want to become a burden to others. It's very common.

Have you ever stepped into someone's life when they are going through a tough time? You took the chance and knocked on their door. The offer to help was received graciously.

Sometimes we assume that people know what we need when we're grieving. Not so. Friends are likely waiting for you to tell them what's helpful.

So, when someone phones you or drops over to offer help in some way, let them know what you need. You might be surprised at how willing they are to help out.

DAY 198
CLOUDS

Keep looking up…that's the secret of life.
—Charles Schulz

It was a beautiful day. Then I looked up at the sky and said to the grandchildren, "Wow, do you see the elephant in that cloud?" They looked at me oddly and then realized what I was doing. "Oh, yeah! Look at that horse over there," one of them continued, pointing to a big cumulus cloud. And others began to imagine animal shapes as well. It was fun and they were pretty creative.

I love cloud-gazing. It's better when you do it together. When you see some formation in the cloud, you want to point it out for others to enjoy before it morphs into something else.

Even in your grief, don't forget to look up. Lift your head. Go for a walk. Breathe deeply and enjoy the clouds.

DAY 199
FINISH

Next year I'm going to be a changed person.
—Charlie Brown, Peanuts

Where's the finish line in grief? There isn't one. Grief will lighten, but it's impossible *not* to miss someone who has impacted your life and contributed to who you are as a person.

You might say to yourself, "It's a new start and a new year. Time to leave the past behind and start fresh." That's true for many things—grudges, weight loss, exercise, SMART goals, etc.

But "leaving the past behind" doesn't apply to grief.

You can't leave the past behind—it includes a person who is still important to you and always will be, whether they are physically present or not.

DAY 200
ALPHABET

I still miss those I loved who are no longer with me, but I find I am grateful for having loved them. The gratitude has finally conquered the loss.
–Rita Mae Brown

I'VE ALWAYS WONDERED why my handwriting is so atrocious—particularly my g's and r's. Recently, I discovered why.

As I watched my granddaughter learn to write, I looked on with amazement as she followed the prescribed direction and order of the lines that made up the letters. I had been writing those letters the wrong way all my life. When I tried it the correct way, following the prompts of my 5-year-old granddaughter, it looked great! It just needed some tweaking.

You are shaped by your past experiences. If someone tells you to forget your loved one and move on, they don't understand. Your loved one helped shape who you are. It's more important to think about how you might remember your loved one in the future.

What tweaks will you make to integrate them into your next chapter in a meaningful way?

DAY 201
FLICKER

*The darker the night, the brighter the stars,
the deeper the grief, the closer is God!*
—FYODOR DOSTOEVSKY

THE CANDLE ON our bistro table was burning low. It flickered, smouldered a little, then it went out completely. I wondered if our server would return and relight it.

Is death like that? Is it really the end? You live then you're gone? Could there be something next? What if…?

While I pondered these things, she came back, lit the candle once again and I said to myself, "Yes! That's it!"

DAY 202
TIPS

*Say not in grief "he is no more" but
live in thankfulness that he was.*
—Hebrew proverb

Tips are a thank-you for good service. For me, it's a way to say, "You made my time here more enjoyable."

Why not take a moment to say "thank you" to the person you miss? Focus on how they made your life more enjoyable.

Maybe as an exercise you could write down all of the things you are thankful for as you reflect upon your relationship with this person. It will help you realize how blessed you were to have had this individual in your life.

It's always a good time to think about what you had and to be grateful, even if what you had is no longer there. Life is just better with gratitude in it.

DAY 203
TSUNAMI

Never above you. Never below you. Always beside you.
—Walter Winchell

We were woken up abruptly at 3:50 a.m. one morning.

The firefighter at our door said, "There is a tsunami warning in effect. You must evacuate the premises within the next hour—don't delay. Here are the directions to the evacuation center." Still bleary-eyed and half asleep, it took me a couple of minutes to get my bearings and realize the implications of what was coming.

Erica and I grabbed a few random things and our computers and left as quickly as we could. It's strange what you think about when the unexpected happens in life. My first thought was: "I sure hope the car starts!"

About an hour later, we returned to our condo—danger averted—all was well again.

Grief comes unexpectedly—and in waves. You can't always predict how it will come crashing into your life or banging on your door, but grief *does* come.

How might we prepare for it?

Expect it. Don't ignore it. Get ready and enter into it as best you can, knowing that it will return at various points in your life and leave again like waves on the shore.

Don't go around grief. Don't let it stop you. There's only one healthy way and that's to step into it.

You will be OK. You really will.

DAY 204
LEARNED

*The life of the dead is placed in
the memory of the living.*
—Marcus Tullius Cicero

WHAT DID YOU learn from _____'s life that you would like to include in your story?

Every person who is important to you has influenced your life in some way.

You are made up of a whole bunch of different people who have had an impact on you. Whether consciously or unconsciously, you have appropriated traits from loved ones and friends who have become part of how you operate.

Many of these *influencers* may have died, but what you've learned from them has not. They have taught you something that you now include in your story in some unique way.

There's part of them in you and now you carry it forward into your own story.

What have you learned from the person who has died? How might you carry it forward into your own life?

DAY 205
WORDS

You are not only responsible for what you say, but also for what you do not say.
—Martin Luther

WORDS ARE POWERFUL.

If you spent time with the person who died, then you can hear their voice and recall their words—phrases they'd repeat often that were important to them and revealed what they valued and who they were.

This person had a way of communicating with you that was unique. Even now, if you take time to think back, you can remember some of the conversations you had that were significant.

Remember these words. Bring your loved one into your life through the words you remember.

DAY 206
LOST

Grief is the price we pay for love.
–Queen Elizabeth II

I lost my cell phone for a few hours the other day and was in a state of panic.

It's my connection to so many people. I feared I was missing important messages from clients, family or friends.

I know, I'm dependant on that little device. I don't like that I'm so attached to it.

I did find it eventually and was relieved. Crisis averted.

We get attached, don't we? That's what we do as human beings. We're built for it.

But even after a loss, a relationship of significance can be found by tapping into the stories of life experience with that person. That can help bring them back to us and remind us of the attachment we had.

DAY 207
ONE

But in all of the sadness, when you're feeling that your heart is empty, and lacking, you've got to remember that grief isn't the absence of love. Grief is the proof that love is still there.
—Tessa Shaffter

It's my birthday tomorrow.

"One more sleep," my youngest grandchild would say. "Yes, one more sleep," I would reply.

Truthfully, we don't know if we are going to have another birthday. None of us knows our future.

In grief, we are just trying to manage one day at a time. *One more sleep* is as far ahead as we can think.

It's okay to take it one day at time and not think too much about the days ahead. Be kind to yourself.

DAY 208
HEALING

There should be a statute of limitation on grief. A rule book that says it is all right to wake up crying, but only for a month. That after forty-two days you will no longer turn with your heart racing, certain you have heard her call out your name. That there will be no fine imposed if you feel the need to clean out her desk; take down her artwork from the refrigerator; turn over a school portrait as you pass—if only because it cuts you fresh again to see it. That it's okay to measure the time she has been gone, the way we once measured her birthdays.
—Jodi Picoult

Healing is a powerful word. If you don't believe you can heal from your grief journey, then you're left with very little hope. There's no clock that ticks and times you as you heal.

Just recognizing that healing is available to you will help you to believe in a future in which your grief is lighter.

DAY 209
46%

Tears are a river that takes you somewhere...
Tears lift your boat off the rocks, off dry ground,
carrying it downriver to someplace better.
—Clarissa Pinkola Estés

I GLANCED AT MY computer battery. It said 46%. The battery icon always stares at me from the top right-hand corner of my computer, reminding me that I need to plug it in at some point. If I don't keep an eye on it, my computer will shut off.

When you are experiencing grief, you are running on empty. There are feelings and situations accosting you from every angle that drain you. Your battery needs serious recharging.

But how do you do that? By spending time with family or friends; treating yourself to a meal out; going to a spa; getting away for a short holiday. You know yourself best.

How do *you* plug in when you're running out of juice?

DAY 210
SUNRISE

*If the present is really all we have,
then the present lasts forever.*
—Anne Lamott

We watch it every morning on the horizon. Orange. Purple. Pink. Gold. We walk away for a moment and return only to see the colours of the sunrise evolve into a new colour palette. Multiple works of art at dawn every day. Beautiful.

It might be hard to see beauty in your world right now. Grief feels like a perpetual drab grey. You may not even be able to see beauty on the horizon.

But I wonder if beauty isn't closer than you think.

DAY 211
CURIOUS QUESTION #10

What does *Deep* say to you about your love for the person who died?

GRIEF REQUIRES DEEP work. It seems odd to use the word *work* when speaking of grief. Sometimes it feels like grief just *is*.

But there's great depth to grief. We can ask questions in our grief journey that can potentially change us and bring a surprising insight. If we don't think about dying well, we won't know how to live well.

Take *Deep* to a different level and ask it a simple question.

- Where are you taking me today that's important?
- What you saying to me that I need to know?

Then listen carefully.

DAY 212
TEACHER

*It all depends on how we look at things,
and not how they are in themselves.*
—Carl Jung

In many ways, grief is a teacher…if we allow it to teach us. It shows us things we may not have known or understood about ourselves; it can help us grow in unexpected ways and reveal areas in our lives that are needing attention.

And that's a good thing.

When you think about it, there are not too many experiences as telling as the grief experience following the death of someone you love dearly.

Nobody welcomes loss in their life, but it is a part of every human's experience. The challenge is whether or not we'll be willing students and let grief teach us what we need to learn.

I wonder what you'll learn today.

DAY 213
SMILE

*Let us always meet each other with a smile,
for the smile is the beginning of love.*
–Mother Teresa

I SMILED AT SOMEONE today when I was at Starbucks and they smiled back. We shared a brief moment of joy—even though we didn't know each other.

It was just a smile—but it warmed my heart.

I make it a practice to smile at people. Even though there are times they don't smile back, it's okay. When I do get a smile back, it's a gift that improves my day.

A smile returned says, "It's a good life. You're okay! You're safe."

If you are grieving, it seems odd to encourage *you* to smile at another person. It's probably the last thing you feel like doing. But what if a smile returned is the exact thing that you really need that day? Maybe you made that other person's day.

Maybe it's worth risking a smile.

DAY 214
YOU

Being deeply loved by someone gives you strength, while loving someone deeply gives you courage.
–Lao Tzu

You're beautiful. You're unique. You deserve to experience joy.

Joy can be restored. Your life can still be filled with moments that are beautiful even though the person whom you miss is not physically present to enjoy them with you.

Keeping this person alive in your heart and mind, bringing them forward for a *visit* when you need them—these are good practices.

It's always what you were given and not what you weren't that is a key to your future joy and continued happiness.

DAY 215
HOPE

*How lucky I am to have something that
makes saying goodbye so hard.*
–Winnie the Pooh

Hope is always about *tomorrow*. When you are grieving, it's difficult to think about tomorrow without that special person in your life.

It's too sad. Too scary. Too unknown.

But Hope calls you out of that place—it needs a chance to speak.

When it does, will you be able to hear what Hope is saying?

DAY 216
INVITE

Grief knits two hearts in closer bonds than happiness ever can; and common sufferings are far stronger links than common joys.
—Alphonse de Lamartine

It's so important to invite the person who has died (and whom you are missing) into your family celebrations. I know that sounds strange.

You will likely need some alone time because of the difficult emotions that accompany the grief you are experiencing during this season. Seeing friends and family all together remind you all the more of who will *not* be at the dinner table at this family celebration.

By giving your loved one a place at your table or in your celebration, you not only honour them, but you also connect with them as best you can, reminding yourself (and others) of how blessed you were to have them in your life.

DAY 217
TABLE

In times of grief and sorrow I will hold you and rock you and take your grief and make it my own. When you cry, I cry and when you hurt, I hurt. And together we will try to hold back the floods of tears and despair and make it through the potholed street of life.
       —Nicholas Sparks, The Notebook

Most tables have four legs. Take one leg away and it's likely to fall over or be unstable at the very least.

When your loved one dies, it feels as though something has been taken out from under you. It has—someone who was a support to you.

You might need someone to lean on for a bit if you feel unbalanced. Who might you ask to be a grief friend?

Maybe you can ask someone who has leaned on you in the past to extend the favor to you. They may be more than happy to be a support to you—now that the table is turned.

DAY 218
CINAMMON BUNS

And in the end, it is not the years in your life that count, it's the life in your years.
—Abraham Lincoln

GRANDMA WASN'T ABLE to visit because she was working, and the grandkids missed her. So, our three-year old grandson, went and got two Ziploc baggies. He took two freshly baked cinnamon buns that his mom had made. "Grandma," he said, pointing to the bun and then slipped it into the bag. "And Pa," he said, wanting to be sure that I had one as well. He smiled up at me.

He wanted to remember Grandma, whom he was missing.

Are you missing someone you love today?

How will you remember them?

DAY 219
PEOPLE

When grief is deepest, words are fewest.
–Ann Voskamp

Relationships with others often change after a person dies.

Prior to the death of your loved one, you had relatives, friends or a community group you belonged to. Some of them supported you for a while, then drifted away. Others didn't engage you in your loss at all, while some friends were with you for the long haul.

Why the difference? Some people are just more comfortable engaging a person who has experienced loss, while others shy away and don't know how to help.

Don't be too hard on people. Try not to be angry or upset with them if they relate to you differently now.

Being grateful for the individuals who have reached out to you will go a long way.

Thank those people for being there for you.

DAY 220
WISDOM

Everything has seasons, and we have to be able to recognize when something's time has passed and be able to move into the next season. Everything that is alive requires pruning as well, which is a great metaphor for endings.
—Henry Cloud

WISDOM COMES AS a result of experience. It's often our *valley* experiences that change us the most. No one likes difficult times.

If grief does anything positive in our lives, it's a bringer of wisdom and resilience. We are going to come out the other side, learn a lot about ourselves, others and the world in which we live. These insights are things we carry with us—even into the next valley, whatever that might be.

What have you learned that is important for you and your future?

DAY 221
SUBJECTIVITY

Do not forsake wisdom, and she will protect you; love her, and she will watch over you. Wisdom is supreme; therefore, get wisdom. Though it cost all you have, get understanding.
—King Solomon

What's inside us is subjective. That's neither good nor bad.

When we say that we are "thinking things through," we are actually "feeling things through" because our thoughts and feelings are co-mingled. Our emotions take over in grief and tend to get a lot more airtime.

We know that we get fuzzy brain as a result of stress, not always thinking clearly. That's why it's important to lay our emotions out on the table and examine them: *What are they really saying to me? Are their messages important for me to consider or not?*

Sometimes we need an objective perspective on this subjective matter.

DAY 222
BELIEVE

*A real friend is one who walks in when
the rest of the world walks out.*
—Walter Winchell

Tell someone that you believe in them.

Are there individuals in your life whom you could empower through your words? Perhaps there's someone who needs you to spur them on to the next important step in their life, someone who could use your encouragement.

Even in the midst of your loss, don't stop building into other important relationships.

People still need you, even if you are grieving.

DAY 223
HOLIDAY

Grief changes shape, but it never ends.
—Keanu Reeves

Have you started planning for your summer holidays yet?

Do you ever plan on grief coming back during these special holiday times? Grief is bound to return during these times—times that in the past have been marked by a family gathering, a vacation or a celebration. But this year, there is someone missing.

Think carefully how you might include your loved one who has died into family events that are important to you. Give that person a place in your day: tell a story, light a candle, bring a photo or display an item that was important to them.

You will be glad you included them in your holiday planning.

DAY 224
SUDDENLY

You said, "Move on." Where do I go?
—Katy Perry

There's a difference between *sudden death* and *dying*.

It has to do with anticipatory grief and loss. In dying, there is time to prepare and talk with your loved one prior to their death.

Whether sudden or on the long haul, death and loss are never easy. In sudden death there's a shock factor that sends cortisol levels skyrocketing.

Our brain's normal reaction is to protect us by sending a signal that releases a hormone that says to our body, "I need help!" Part of the "fight or flight" phenomenon, cortisol is necessary but can be damaging too.

Elevated stress is part of all grief. Managing it with healthy interventions is key to staying well—mentally and physically—in the midst of grief.

DAY 225
COOKIES

I am because you were.
—Unknown

Our daughter, Larissa, understands the importance of tradition and how it applies to grief.

So, she started a new tradition. She bakes Christmas cookies with her stepmom, Erica. Many of the cookie recipes are the same ones that she and her mom, Pam, used to make together, while a number of the recipes are ones that Erica introduced to the family. There's always one new recipe that's unfamiliar to them both.

Larissa misses Pam but connects with her by making cookies.

Connection through food is a powerful tool for remembering a loved one.

DAY 226
PLAY

It's very hard to find your own words—and you don't actually exist until you have your own words.
—Jordan Peterson

CHILDREN TEACH ADULTS how to play. Being "grown up" and forgetting how to have fun isn't a good thing.

In grief, "play" is particularly important for our mental health. Whatever play looks like to you, if you engage in it, it will fire up neurochemicals that can bring joy back into your life following loss.

Having a tough grief day?

Go and find a child or grandchild to hang out with. Then go out and play.

DAY 227
MIRROR

The reality is that you will grieve forever. You will not "get over" the loss of a loved one; you will learn to live with it. You will heal and you will rebuild yourself around the loss you have suffered. You will be whole again, but you will never be the same. Nor should you be the same nor would you want to.
—Elisabeth Kübler-Ross & David Kessler

GRIEF IS LIKE a mirror. It reflects back to you what you need to learn about yourself in relation to others.

This is not always easy as we are such complex beings. Are there some things you're seeing in your grief that will help you grow as an individual? Things in your life that are restricting your joy and relationships with others? Are there some wrinkles you're seeing in that mirror that could be mitigated?

Grief is looking straight at you and asking you some questions. Don't back away from the mirror. Just ask, "What do I need to know about myself today?"

Let grief be your teacher.

DAY 228
HOME

I like to stop and count my blessings.
–Ziggy

"There's no place like home!" says Dorothy in the *Wizard of Oz*, longing to go back to Kansas to be with her family.

But what if the person who makes that home special is no longer there?

It's a different home now, isn't it?

I did not like walking into my home following the death of my first wife. It felt so empty without her.

Then the kids would come home, and friends would visit, and I'd realize that home is a place filled with people who love me and with whom I share life.

It was only then that I realized I would be okay—in my home.

DAY 229
UPGRADED

Spread love everywhere you go. Let no one ever come to you without leaving happier.
—Mother Theresa

We ended up in first class and I have no idea know why. The plane was very full but somehow, we were the ones selected for an upgrade.

Water and snacks were already at our seats–bigger seats with lots of leg room. The flight attendant came and asked us if we wanted some extra snacks and drinks. My wife said, "Is there a cost?" "No, it's all free with your priority ticket," she replied. We felt like royalty.

If you know someone who has experienced the death of someone special, why not give them some extra attention and make them a priority in your life for a bit?

Your kind gesture might be the unexpected surprise that makes their day a little more manageable.

DAY 230
FLY

*If tears could build a stairway, and memories a lane,
I'd walk right up to heaven and bring you home again.*
—Unknown

"I wonder where it's flying to?" we asked each other as we watched the plane fly high above us and disappear out of sight. We all took a creative guess at where it might be going. It was fun to hear the various destinations everyone was choosing to fly to if they had the choice.

"I wonder where my loved one is?" That's a question I've heard many times in my grief practice as a counsellor. I usually reply, "Where do *you* think?" and we have a conversation about the possibilities.

It seems that most people find a lot of peace in the hope that their loved one is on another journey—that somehow amid the mystery of life, there is in fact something next.

It becomes even more amazing to consider the idea that you might see this person again.

What would you say to them person if you met them for the first time again after you had died?

DAY 231
DREAMS

You can clutch the past so tightly to your chest that it leaves your arms too full to embrace the present.
—Jan Gildwell

It's hard to fathom the beginning of another year without your loved one. Or perhaps you are looking forward to turning the page on this past year that's been so tough.

Whichever it is, you may want to look back on your year and examine how it impacted your life:

- Did you do the things you set out to do?
- Will you do things differently this year?

If this is the first time you are entering a new year without that someone special who has died, try inviting them into your year.

How do you do that? I wonder what hopes and dreams your loved one would wish for you. Can you hear their words of encouragement to you?

DAY 232
CURIOUS QUESTION #11

In what way might you bring joy to another person's life today?

WHY SHOULD *I bring joy to another when I feel so sad?* Because you are a joy-giver, not a kill joy. People need you just as much as you need them.

When you bring joy to another person's life, you reap the benefits without even realizing it. That's what neuroscientists have discovered about our brains—that oxytocin is released when we give and receive love. That's the hormone that makes us feel joyful.

Love and joy are emotions we can all use more of.

How might you bring joy today? Who might need a little extra attention?

DAY 233
DEEP

*Some people come in your life as blessings.
Some come in your life as lessons.*
—Mother Teresa

Our three-year-old grandson ran out into the ocean with reckless abandon.

My first thought was, "Wow! He's so brave!" My second thought was, "Yikes! That water gets deep quickly!"

We ran in after him, fearful that his momentum and the deep swell of the waves would make for a deadly combination. We scooped him up just before the water became too deep and engulfed him.

Of course, he did it again! No fear. But this time we watched him more closely, ready to avert any danger.

Who is watching over you when you get in over your head and you feel as though the swell will take you under?

You may want to invite another person to check in on you once in a while to make sure you're not in too deep.

DAY 234
TOMATOES

People grow through experience if they meet life honestly and courageously. This is how character is built.
—Eleanor Roosevelt

Tomatoes are one of my favourite fruits. You read it right: tomatoes aren't vegetables, they're classified as a fruit.

Why aren't tomatoes considered a vegetable? Because they come from seed-bearing organisms that develop from a flowering plant. Vegetables, on the other hand, are roots, stems, leaves or other auxiliary parts of a plant.

I think of grief as a single seed that grows from within us. If watered and cared for, it will result in a flower that bears good fruit—perhaps different from what we were expecting. Grief is not just a root that needs to be pulled from the dark earth.

Grief is like a tomato.

DAY 235
SPICE

Food is symbolic of love when words are inadequate.
–ALAN D WOLFELT

I TASTED THE BEST spice ever the other day. I had never heard of it before. Someone told me about it.

"How did I not know about this spice?" I said to myself. Happy to know about it now, I'm telling everyone else about my new-found discovery.

Hearing someone else's grief story can be very helpful. Even though you are unique in the way you process grief, hearing another's grief story helps you see that what you're experiencing is normal. Seeing people who've lived through grief and come out the other side brings hope.

Stories are the spice of life. You might want to ask another person about the person they are missing. When they share their story, be open to the possibility of sharing yours too.

DAY 236
TAXI

Who looks outside, dreams; who looks inside, awakes.
—CARL JUNG

HE PICKED ME up to take me to the airport. "You can sit in the back," he said to me. "I'd like to sit in the front, if that's okay with you," I replied. He shuffled a few items on the seat next to him and I hopped into the passenger seat.

I often choose the front seat of a taxi because I like to engage the driver in conversation.

I wonder if we need to move Grief from the back seat to the passenger seat in order to intentionally engage it in conversation.

What do you have to say to Grief today? And what might you share about your grief journey with the person next to you?

DAY 237
PRAY

*God gave us memory so that we might
have roses in December.*
–J. M. Barrie

SEEKING A *HIGHER power* has been beneficial to many during grief. There are times when we need to believe that there's something bigger than ourselves. Praying is a way of showing you believe this to be true.

Many people review their connection with God in their grief journey. What do you do when you have deep questions and no apparent answers on the horizon? Do you look beyond yourself? If you do, I wonder if there might be someone who is listening and ready to respond.

Prayer is communication—a two-way street.

You might want to explore the spiritual dimension of grief.

DAY 238
PROTECT

The risk of love is loss, and the price of loss is grief. But the pain of grief is only a shadow when compared with the pain of never risking love.
—Hillary Stanton Zunin

Vulnerable people need protecting.
When grief first hits, you are vulnerable and exhausted. So much to do, so many changes in your life and your emotions are in flux.

What do you do with a broken heart?

You fill it up with love.

Open yourself up to love and be loved.

DAY 239
READY

You can never really live anyone else's life, not even your child's. The influence you exert is through your own life, and what you've become yourself.
—Eleanor Roosevelt

Is anyone really ready when a loved one dies? Even if we think we're ready, we're never really prepared for the emotional responses that come as a result of having someone close to us die.

Grief always surprises us in some way.

I don't enjoy grief, but I know it wants to say something to me that might be important. So, perhaps being ready might mean listening to its deeper message about my own life.

DAY 240
GIFT

Of all Sad Words of Tongue or Pen, the Saddest are these, "It Might Have Been."
—George Ade, More Fables

"You're a gift to me."

Would you consider the person you are missing this holiday season as a gift that you were given? Look at your life with them and thank them for being part of it.

True, they are no longer with you—that's very hard. They were part of your family celebrations.

In the midst of missing them, you can still say: "You were a gift to me. Thank you for being part of my life."

Perhaps you might unwrap a little of their story, sharing it at your family event. Celebrate what they gave you in your life—blessings for which you are thankful.

DAY 241
PACE

Things we lose have a way of coming back to us in the end, if not always in the way we expect.
—J. K. ROWLING,
HARRY POTTER AND THE ORDER OF THE PHOENIX

IT'S ALWAYS A question of load versus capacity. Pacing yourself.

That's true for the muscles in your body. It's also true for your emotional well-being following a loss.

Are you trying to move on too quickly? Throwing out everything that reminds you of your loved one? Moving homes? Getting remarried right away? Chucking old photos?

What are you running from? Grief will catch up to you.

Take time to love and miss.

Why not *ask* the person who has died to accompany you on your grief journey?

They may have some wisdom to share with you—and allow you to pace yourself as you move into your next life chapter.

DAY 242
SONG

Music is the moonlight in the gloomy night of life.
—Jean Paul Friedrich Richter

Music is a powerful medium that brings us back to the person who has died. It seems that most people I talk to about grief, conclude that there are songs that were special and bring back memories of their loved one.

Grief returns through a song—so do memories. Happy and sad tears all at the same time.

Do you have a special song that connects you to someone who has died? What happens when you hear it played on the radio? How do you feel? Will you stop for a moment to remember?

What songs do you remember and why?

DAY 243
MESSAGE

Life has to end. Love doesn't.
—Mitch Albom

IF YOU WERE able to send a message to your loved one who died to tell them how you were doing, what would your loved one want to hear from you?

If your loved one was able to send you a message, what would they say to you?

You still have a relationship with the person who has died, even if it's not in person.

You spent time together. You know what they'd say to you. I'm almost certain you could hear what words they would speak to you. I wonder if writing down those words might be helpful to you.

DAY 244
APPRECIATE

I would maintain that thanks are the highest form of thought; and that gratitude is happiness doubled by wonder.
—G. K. Chesterton

Tell someone you appreciate them.

Are there people in your life who are important to you? Have you ever told them why they are important to you?

Maybe it's time.

DAY 245
INTENTIONAL

*In tough times, that's when you see
the true colors and personality.*
—Didier Deschamps

A SMALL GET-TOGETHER WITH a friend or two? A large event with lots of people? That will depend on whether you're an introvert or an extrovert. The number of people only matters in terms of your preference.

Whether many or few, it's a good idea to spend time with people in your grief journey. Even if you're an introvert, going it alone isn't always the best response to your grief.

You don't have to wait for an invitation. Be intentional. Let people know you would like to spend time with them.

Sometimes people just don't know when you are ready. But you do.

DAY 246
HOUSE

If we have no peace, it is because we have forgotten that we belong to each other.
—Mother Teresa

It's more than four walls—it's the place where memories are formed. That's why it can be a difficult place to live in your grief journey.

It's a challenge to resist the temptation to change things up around the house following loss—everything reminds you of your loved one.

The flipside is wanting everything to remain untouched because you feel it's dishonoring to the person. You choose not to move or change anything for fear it might send a message to someone else who had memories in that house. So, you live in a proverbial museum.

Perhaps there is a happy medium: Remember the good memories that connect you with that person and keep those items that allow you to hold your loved one close.

DAY 247
COFFEE

*Grieving doesn't make you imperfect.
It makes you human.*
—Sarah Dessen

When you walk into a specialty coffee shop, the options seem limitless. You can enjoy your favourite latte, dark roast or Americano the way you want it. They've got your coffee preference covered. The sky is the limit for choice.

You have preferences in how you manage your grief as well. Each person is unique. You'll grieve the death of a loved one differently than another person would.

Not being sensitive to each other's needs and preferences when grieving can lead to conflict.

DAY 248
FRUIT

Each one of us fulfills a piece of a larger puzzle.
–Eric McCormack

WE PICKED THE last of the blackberries for the season. We'd have to wait until next year to enjoy the next batch.

When someone dies, we tend to think that it's the last of them (unless of course your worldview suggests that there's something next). Even then, when people die, we tend to believe they are no longer in our lives.

I would disagree.

The fruit of the lives of our loved ones who have died spill out into us. If we choose to graft them into our story as we move forward, they will always bear fruit in the garden of our lives.

DAY 249
ERASER

One cannot and must not try to erase the past merely because it does not fit the present.
–Golda Meir

It's good to be able to erase a mistake and get rid of it for good.

However, it bothers me when people say that they need to forget the person who died and "move on with their life"—as if you could simply erase them and move forward with a blank slate. To *erase* someone from your life is impossible—they've been grafted into you.

You and I are made up of a whole bunch of different people. What part of this person will remain on your chalk board forever?

DAY 250
TRAVEL

You know you love someone when you cannot put into words how they make you feel.
–Margaret Mead

"Where should we travel next?"

Lost dreams in grief are so tough. So many plans for the future fade quickly into the dark of night. Gone forever. How do you grapple with these losses when they sit in front of you? How do you manage the days that follow?

Perhaps remembering the travels that you *did* have together and giving thanks for the dreams you *did* share is the best you can do.

DAY 251
FORGIVE

*Forgiveness does not change the past,
but it does enlarge the future.*
—Paul Boose

Tell someone you forgive them.

Is there a person you have not seen for a long time but need to see? Is the reason you haven't seen them because of something that has happened in the past that has put a block between the two of you? Does your relationship with them need a *reboot*?

Forgiveness is a good start point.

DAY 252
BRINGING

Kind words not only lift our spirits in the moment they are given, but they can linger with us over the years.
—Joseph B. Wirthlin

There are many of life's celebrations for which we'd love to bring back a deceased loved one.

Do you ever find yourself in the middle of a celebration missing that person? Do you, even for a moment, wish they would walk through that door and greet you? Do you long to hear their words of encouragement just one more time? Do you wish you could see them smile at you as you celebrate this pivotal moment in your life?

If you are like me, then your answer is *yes* to all of the above.

But you *can* invite your loved one to be part of your celebration and ongoing story even though they are not physically present. There is a simple strategy that will bring your loved one closer—it begins with a question: *What would they say to me today if they were present?*

DAY 253
CURIOUS QUESTION #12

Where do you place *Fear* when it tries to take away your joy?

BEING ABLE TO identity emotion that stifle your joy is a crucial step as you adapt and move forward.

It's normal to be concerned about your future and wonder what's next without this special person in your life, but *Fear* can be debilitating.

It's hard to articulate what *Fear* does—other than take up a lot of mental real-estate that could otherwise be dedicated to more life-giving thoughts.

Have a conversation with *Fear* today if it's troubling you. It could go like this: "Hey you, *Fear*! You can't scare me. Sure, there are some unknowns right now, but you're not going to tell me who I am or what my future is. So, move over. I have a new friend named *Joy* coming for a visit."

DAY 254
MOUNTAIN

Over every mountain there is a path, although it may not be seen from the valley.
—Theodore Roethke

Mountains are so majestic. Each one is unique. I could study them for hours.

I have been on a few mountain peaks—the journey to the top made the climb worthwhile. What a view—spectacular! I couldn't help but marvel in wonder at the beauty.

And I'm always amazed at how I can look in every direction and see far into the distance. It gives me a whole new perspective on the world.

While you might not consider grief to be a *mountaintop experience*, what perspective is grief giving you on the world?

DAY 255
FISHING

Although it's difficult today to see beyond the sorrow, may looking back in memory help comfort you tomorrow.
—Unknown

"I LOVE GOING FISHING. Every year, some of us guys would fly to an isolated cabin on a lake and fish together," he said to me. "What's your best fishing story?" I asked. "Oh, it has nothing to do with fishing," he replied. "It's is more about the bear who wandered into our cabin to get the fish we'd caught," he chortled.

He had me enthralled as he recounted the rest of his crazy "fishing" adventure with his buddies.

Adventures and experiences. They are a healthy part of remembering and need to be shared, especially in the midst of a grief journey.

What's your favourite story about your loved one or friend who has died? Does it make you smile, cry or evoke a feeling of gratitude that you had them in your life?

DAY 256
FORK

A river cuts through rock, not because of its power, but because of its persistence.
–Jim Watkins

I WONDER IF YOU'VE ever experienced a fork in the road on your journey with grief. "Oh, just a few!" you might reply.

You may feel that you've had a myriad of decisions foisted on you following a loss.

I've often heard clients say, "I don't have any direction in my life. I'm not sure which way to turn."

Having to make too many decisions at once can overwhelm you and cause you to spin your wheels.

One of the side effects of loss is *grief brain*, which makes decision-making even more challenging. So, you'll need to take it easy and give yourself a break. Deal with each fork in the road as it comes and don't let multiple decisions burden you.

DAY 257
DRIFTWOOD

The risk of love is loss, and the price of loss is grief, but the pain of grief is only a shadow when compared with the pain of never risking love.
—Hilary Stanton Zunin

I LOVE WALKING ALONG the ocean. I especially love looking at all the driftwood washed up on the shore. Where did it all come from? Where has it been? How long was it adrift in the ocean? Each piece has a different story. I always look for signs that might indicate the bigger story behind that piece of driftwood.

Was it part of someone's home?

Was it part of a ship?

Did it come from a different part of the world?

To whom did that piece of wood belong?

Each of us has a story—honed for a purpose and for ongoing connection. Your loved one may no longer be with you, but their story needs to be remembered.

In your grief, beware of cutting your loved one adrift. They are still impactful even when they are gone. As you walk through life, you take them with you because they have become part of your ongoing story.

How has your loved one had an impact on your own narrative?

DAY 258
BINGO

In the book of life, the answers aren't in the back.
—Charles Schulz

You wait for your number to be called and you win the prize. I won a lamp at a bingo game once. I was twelve years old. I still remember the excitement of winning.

Some people who die are ready to die. They've lived a long life and have finished the race. They feel that dying would be like *winning the prize*. Others who are dying wish they could live longer—their choice would have been to have more time on this earth. They weren't finished living.

Regardless of the scenario, those of us who are left behind still grieve and still miss.

DAY 259
PLAN

The only cure for grief is action.
—George Henry Lewes

It's good to have a plan.

Plans can change but at least making a plan can give you some measure of control in a world that's always fluctuating due to grief.

One step forward can empower you.

What's one thing you can plan to do today to help you in your grief journey? It doesn't need to be a big thing—just something that will take the edge off the chaos.

DAY 260
OSTEOPATHY

Grief can be a burden, but also an anchor. You get used to the weight, how it holds you in place.
—Sarah Dessen, The Truth About Forever

I HAD SEVERE PAIN in my hip. So, I went to the osteopath. I'd never been before as it seemed a little too *out there* for me. But I decided to go on the recommendation of a friend.

I had expected a *no pain, no gain* approach to my treatment, but was pleasantly surprised when, instead of cracking and deep muscle pressure, the osteopath used gentle motions to adjust my aching hip. I left her office with a spring in my step.

When grief hits you hard, be gentle with yourself. Resilience isn't created by muscling through your pain. Gentle adjustments work best over the long haul.

DAY 261
SHARING

And above all these, put on love, which binds everything together in perfect harmony.
—Colossians 3:14

WHEN SOMEONE DIES, those who are left behind share a common grief journey. Why? Because each one had a relationship with the one who died. Perhaps it was a good relationship for one person, but not so positive for another.

When you speak with another person about your grief, it may seem odd that you are experiencing grief differently from someone else. Your take on it isn't the same.

In grief, there is always a tension between what you had and what you wished you had in your relationship with the deceased. That will differ from person to person.

DAY 262
IMPRESSION

Although it's difficult today to see beyond the sorrow, my looking back in memory help comfort you tomorrow.
—Unknown

My bad. I left a mark on the table. I should have used a coaster before I set down that hot drink. It left a ring, a lasting impression on the end table. I left something behind that everyone will see in the future.

We all leave a lasting impression behind. What has your loved one left behind that you are thankful for and that you will remember forever?

What significant story about them has left an indelible mark on your life—one that you will never forget and never want to?

Why not share that story with someone today? It may leave a lasting impression on them.

DAY 263
RETURN

*You can complain that roses have thorns;
or rejoice that thorns have roses.*
—Ziggy

D<small>ON'T BE FRIGHTENED</small> or upset when grief returns. You may feel sadness because you know that you won't be able to experience this person's physical presence in your life any longer—that's hard to manage.

What might be important about grief when it cycles back into your life?

- When did it come?
- What happened emotionally when it returned?
- Was it a place, an event, a picture, an object, or a song that brought this person back to you?
- Did you share this grief experience with another person?

If this grief experience comes back again, it may connect you with them in the future. That's not such a bad thing.

DAY 264
NOVEL

*When someone you love becomes a memory,
that memory becomes a treasure.*
–Unknown

Their story needs to be honored. Your loved one who has died.

Often people will say that you need to transition (quickly) into your new life. "You need to let go of the one who is no longer in your life," is a common phrase or sentiment. Some may even suggest that it's unhealthy to keep them alive in your thoughts.

Finding an enduring connection with this person by including them in your next chapter is likely a better way to go.

How might this person be a part of your *novel* in the future?

DAY 265
HONESTY

Those things that hurt instruct.
—Benjamin Franklin

Honesty is so important in our grief journey. It has a big impact on our behaviour. How is that?

I think all of us have noticed people who have changed following the death of someone special in their life. We often chalk it up to grief and let it slide.

But I really caution you about *letting things slide*. Vulnerability and accountability are key in nipping things in the bud before they get out of hand. Like most of life—it's still about making choices.

Find one person in your life whom you trust and have them ask you this one question each week to help you stay on track: *Have you noticed anything different in my behavior that concerns you?*

This may seem like hard work, but the foundation you lay by asking this simple question will position you well to move through your grief journey.

It will also honour the person who has died. They would be proud of you for doing it.

DAY 266
CALENDAR

You cut off the capacity for grief in your life and you cut off the capacity for joy at the same time. They both come up through the same tunnel. You don't have one without the other.
—WILLIAM HURT

WHEN MY FIRST wife died, I wanted time to stop. I could not imagine living one day without her in my life. I didn't want to think about the next day. It was too painful.

But time didn't stop. Another day came and went, then a week and then a month passed. All I could think was, "Isn't time a gift?" Pam wasn't given more time on this earth. But I was.

That question eventually helped me become thankful for my day, even though there were some really tough ones. I began to say, "I have been given another day on the calendar. I must use it as best I can."

DAY 267
RE-ROUTED

Relax…Tomorrow is the first day of your life too.
—Ziggy

Old GPS systems used to say "recalculating" when you took a wrong turn. Now they just show you that you are being re-routed.

Grief feels a lot like being re-routed.

You think that you are heading in a direction that will help you adjust to your new life without a special person who has died. Then you're re-routed to a different road: "Turn here. Make a U-Turn. Go down this road instead."

Sometimes you want to take an easier road, a shortcut, with the fewest obstacles possible. The reality is that you need to experience the pain of missing that special person.

Feeling is part of being human—joy and sorrow.

While you may not welcome grief, it is part of your missing which is ultimately linked to your love for the person who has died.

It's okay to take the longer route.

DAY 268
LONELY

You never know when a moment and a few sincere words can have an impact on a life.
—Zig Ziglar

Are You Lonesome Tonight? That old song title has new meaning in loss.

It would be strange if you weren't lonely. You may even resent those who try to make you feel happy or push you prematurely into social settings that don't feel right.

Someone has died. Someone you miss. Feeling lonesome is normal.

What would happen if you shared your lonely feelings with one trusted person, telling them what you miss most about that special person who is no longer with you?

DAY 269
MENU

Give the sorrow words; the grief that does not speak knits up the over wrought heart and bids it break.
—William Shakespeare, Macbeth

When I go to a restaurant, I prefer a menu with just a few choices as opposed to one that overwhelms me. If there are too many items from which to choose, I find it difficult to decide and keep changing my mind.

I wonder if, like a menu, people experience so much overwhelm at the outset of their grief journey that they don't know what choices to make.

Often the *grief menu* contains so many details—big and small—that need to be worked through eventually.

Just remind yourself that it's one bite at a time. Don't choke on the details.

DAY 270
MISSING

Death ends a life, not a relationship.
–Mitch Albom

"How are you doing? How are you feeling?"

These are common questions, but perhaps ones that you're tired of answering over and over again as you mourn the loss of someone. Maybe you've even replied that you're "fine," to spare yourself and the other person the discomfort of your sadness.

But perhaps there's a different way of responding that is helpful to both of you. Why not ask this question: "Can I tell you something I really miss about _today?"

With that conversation starter you teach the other person talk about what's really on your mind and in your heart—the person that you miss.

And then, if it's appropriate, you can follow it up with something to engage them:

"So, what do *you* miss most about___?"

DAY 271
PAINFUL

And perhaps there is a limit to the grieving that the human heart can do. As when one adds salt to a tumbler of water, there comes a point where simply no more will be absorbed.
—Sarah Waters

I wish I could fast-forward chronological time. I didn't choose loss—it's really painful.

We want to fast-forward to the part of the story that doesn't include grief. Grief is a really tough place to be.

But experiencing the pain of grief is so necessary since it says to you, "You really miss that person, don't you?"

DAY 272
RUSH

Patience is not simply the ability to wait, it's how we behave while we're waiting.
—Joyce Meyer

When you rush, you...

- make mistakes
- miss out on what is right in front of you that might be important
- create anxiety in and around you
- don't give space for the learning
- don't see what is good
- can't reframe because you are focused on one thing only

Better to be the tortoise than the hare. No need to rush—your grief isn't going anywhere fast.

DAY 273
SMOKE

Hope fills the holes of the frustration in my heart.
—Emanuel Cleaver

I LONGED FOR THE smoke to dissipate. It irritated my throat and stung my eyes. The forest fires were impacting how I lived life. The smoke was dense and hung in the air—over most of Western Canada actually.

I really missed going for walks and being outdoors. I was used to some of the cleanest air on the planet, but last week it was deemed the worst.

Grief is the same. It forces us inside–hiding our inner pain or cutting us off from the world. Grief is suffocating. It stings. It hovers.

Grief can be dense, requiring us to trust that there is life beyond the clouded veil that obstructs our view. Are there really mountain tops beyond what I can see here in this valley?

Then the wind came, and the smoke cleared. I went outside. I breathed. Clean, fresh air filled my lungs. I could see the mountains.

I was ok.

DAY 274
CURIOUS QUESTION #13

**Where do you find peace when
your mind is troubled?**

YOUR MIND CAN play games with you as you transition through grief. Is there a place in your mind where you can go in order to get some rest?

A good start is to write down your thoughts and biggest concerns. Have a conversation with these thoughts and prioritize them in order of importance.

Focus on one thing. Allow your mind to get some rest by leaving the other things for another day.

In short:

1. Write them down.
2. Focus on one.
3. Leave the others for another day.

DAY 275
WALK

You taught me to run, you taught me to fly. Helped me to free the me inside.
—Gloria Estefan

WALK. DON'T RUN.
There are so many ways to walk: casual stroll, strut, shuffle, power walk to name a few.

When we encourage people to *walk* in their grief journey, there's a good reason for it. It's not a race. There's no finish line.

Some types of grief will always be part of your life as you move forward following the death of a loved one.

There's good reason for grief to return—you will miss that person at times in your life and that's okay. When you miss someone, you are missing not only the person but also the relationship you had that was important to you. Hopefully it was one filled with love—and if missing is linked to love, why run quickly past those moments of your life?

Why not slow down and embrace these moments as significant? Why not savor them instead?

So, don't run away from your grief when it returns—it might be the very thing that keeps you walking forward.

DAY 276
WEATHER

Even though the ship may go down, the journey goes on.
—Margaret Mead

"You don't like the weather? Wait five minutes." Living on the West Coast with its changeable weather patterns, I hear that all the time.

Just like the weather, our own emotions can take us by surprise. They shift so quickly, especially when we're grieving. It can even make us question our sanity.

Feelings are there to tell us that we are alive and attempting to sort out what we are experiencing that is difficult for us. Unpleasant emotions are part of life.

So, don't panic. You've got this.

DAY 277
HAMMER

Memory is a way of holding on to the things you love, the things you are, the things you never want to lose.
—The Wonder Years

"Ouch!" I missed the nail and hit my finger. I was so careful, but somehow, I still missed.

No matter how hard you try, you will experience tough moments in your grief journey when you don't do it well. Just know that this is part and parcel of the road that you are on.

You are constructing a different life and whether you are building it intentionally or it is coming to you naturally, there are bound to be times that slow you down and have you saying, "Ouch! I missed!"

When that happens, take a break. You can always go back to building again once you are ready.

DAY 278
HIPPO

For myself I am an optimist—it does not seem to be much use to be anything else.
–Winston Churchill

THEY'RE HUGE! I saw one at the zoo the other day with my grandson.

We watched it through the glass as it swam under water. I kept waiting for the hippo to resurface to take a breath. I couldn't believe how long it could go without air before lifting its enormous head above the water. We waited and waited and waited. It took so long, we finally decided to leave and go to see some other amazing animals.

Many people have described their grief to me as the sensation of being under water and desperately trying to find some fresh air to breathe.

Grief can be suffocating at the outset. But be patient—it won't last forever.

Later we returned to the hippo's tank. It was sunbathing lazily, taking in the fresh air, barely aware of us spectators.

DAY 279
KEY

I started out on the highway way of life and somehow, I ended up on a cow path.
—Ziggy

IT USED TO be that if you lost your house key, the only way into your home was through the window or by busting down the door.

Today, there are other options...

Maybe you have a keyless entry system and—as long as that works properly—you can always get into your home.

Or perhaps you hid a key somewhere for such occasions.

Maybe you left an extra key with a trusted neighbor?

Gone are the days when you could leave your front door unlocked, knowing that your home would be safe while you were away.

Wouldn't it be great if there were a *master grief key* that could unlock every sadness?

Unfortunately, there's not. Each of us is unique and opening up the door to your grief journey is individual and personal.

Who holds that key?

DAY 280
OCEAN

Life is like the ocean—it goes up and down.
–Vanesssa Paradis

WHEN YOU LOOK out at the ocean, you don't always see the far shore—just the horizon.

You know there is land out there somewhere as you journey. You look for landmarks to give you hope that you'll arrive soon. Safely, you hope.

Are there signs in your grief journey telling you that you'll make it through, that you'll be okay?

When you begin to experience small moments of joy, rest assured that you're on course and your grief experience is taking a turn for the better.

DAY 281
SWALLOW

You have the sun, you have the moon, you have the air that you breathe—and you have the Rolling Stones.
–Keith Richards

WHEN I was a kid, I used to sing, *Just a Spoonful of Sugar Makes the Medicine Go Down*. That was before medicine came in various fruit flavours to make it more palatable.

No matter how you take it, it's hard to swallow grief. Reflecting upon how blessed you were to have that person in your life—even though it wasn't long enough—can make the grieving process a little easier to swallow.

When grief takes you down, stop, breathe and ask this simple question:

What three things about my loved one made my life sweeter?

Okay, I hear you say, "Only three?" Well, it's a start.

Time to get out the pen and paper.

DAY 282
ATTITUDE

With the new day comes new strength and new thoughts.
—Eleanor Roosevelt

"What a beautiful day," my wife said to a woman in her fitness class. "The grass and trees are so lush and green!" Winter in Victoria—it rarely snows, but it can get a little rainy. "Yeah, now I have to go home and mow my lawn!" the woman retorted to my wife.

Attitude is everything as you begin your grief journey.

Grief can weigh you down. That's pretty normal. You feel as though you are in a dark place as you live with the sadness.

Practicing gratitude and finding something positive in your day, despite your grief, can go a long way to bringing some light into your darkness and creating hope for your future.

DAY 283
CHANGE

*When one person is missing the
whole world seems empty.*
−Pat Schweibert

It's normal that your relationships will change following the death of a loved one.

You can probably name some relationships that have changed, become different or have grown distant since your loved one died.

I've often looked back on relationships and realized that sometimes people just change, and I don't have much choice how that plays out.

In other relationships, I do have a choice. The relationship might change, but I *can* respond pro-actively. If it's important to me, I will pursue the relationship. Even though it might take extra effort on my part.

DAY 284
FAST

Life seems sometimes like nothing more than a series of losses, from beginning to end. That's the given. How you respond to those losses, what you make of what's left, that's the part you have to make up as you go.
—Katharine Weber

"Come on, Grandpa! Let's have a race!" Jake said. "You're so fast!" I panted after he beat me to the finishing line. Jake smiled. "Come on, Grandpa. Let's go again!" I could feel my hip pain flare up and said, "How about we go fishing instead?" "Okay," Jake conceded.

Distraction is an excellent tool when you want to do something different.

When your grief is taking you in a direction that you'd rather not go—because it's much too fast and it hurts you—stop and decide to do something different.

It really doesn't matter what you do as long as it's healthy and helpful. Just do it.

Say to Grief, "No! I'm not going in that direction today. I'm going this way. Goodbye!"

See you later, alligator!

DAY 285
STILL

*The more you know yourself, the more patience
you have for what you see in others.*
—Erik Erikson

I LOVE BEING STILL. The practice of being still has to be intentional in today's busy and distracting world. We all recognize that. The psalmist wrote, "Be still and know that I am God." I wonder if there is an opportunity to find God in stillness. Is that something worth exploring in your grief journey?

There is so much mystery in life, but we gloss over it when we rush and give into distraction.

What might stillness look like in your day today? Perhaps there's value in sitting quietly, going for a walk by yourself or letting something come to you in the silence.

DAY 286
BEHAVIOUR

Your friends will know you better in the first minute you meet than your acquaintances will know you in a thousand years.
—Richard Bach

Anything that you are either doing more of or less of since your loved one died is up for examination in your grief journey.

Ask a friend if there is anything that they have noticed about you that troubles them. What are they observing? Is there a blind spot in your life?

Seek wisdom from a trusted friend—someone you know will speak truth into your life.

DAY 287
BOTH

A good laugh heals a lot of hurts.
—Madeleine L'Engle

When my friend and I hang out, we tease each other incessantly. Banter and laughter have always been a big part of our friendship.

It doesn't stop there though—we also have some pretty intense discussions as well. We make time for that too.

There's room for both types of interactions in your grief journey—a time to be serious and a time to laugh.

It's okay to laugh. It's okay to be serious. Both are necessary.

DAY 288
DAYS

*How lucky I am to have something that
makes saying goodbye so hard.*
–A.A. Milne

DAYS—A DIFFICULT WORD when it's plural and you're on a journey with grief. One day is more than enough when you are grieving. Looking too far ahead prevents you from living in *this* day.

Consider being present with your thoughts and feelings today. If you allow your heart and mind to run ahead, you risk being overwhelmed by grief and any of its accompanying emotions.

"Live in the present"—we hear it all the time. It's a tough discipline to actually *do*. The trick is to be open and grateful for what you have in your life *today*, despite missing someone who meant the world to you.

What's good in this 24-hour day?

DAY 289
SNOW

Time is no longer endless or the horizon destitute of hope.
—Charles Lindbergh

I sat beside her on the plane. She was so excited to see the snow. She had never experienced it before.

As she peered out the window at the brightness, her eyes widened and with a big smile, she turned to face me, revealing the childlike joy in her eyes.

Something new! Something she had never experienced before.

For me, snow was commonplace. All I could think about was having to shovel it off my driveway and scrape it from my windshield.

Looking out a different window—or at least looking out the same window with different eyes—in the midst of your grief journey can be difficult. But so necessary.

Life always has something to give if you can view it with a different set of eyes.

DAY 290
IN-BETWEEN

*There are things known and things unknown
and in between are the doors*
−Jim Morrison

The "in-between time" is a big deal in grief. I often hear, "How long will this grief last?"

I believe that what people are really saying is: "How long between the time I desperately miss my loved one to the time when I might actually have a day that's not so sad and lonely?"

Grief *does* lighten and we must not feel like we're dishonoring the person who has died when we have a good day.

The "in-between time" is important in your grief journey. Only you will know when it needs to include a "what's next?"

DAY 291
HUMAN

The only reason for time is so that everything doesn't happen at once.
—Albert Einstein

To be human is to hurt. No one chooses pain, tears or sorrow. But it's part and parcel of being human. No one has a "pass" on life's losses. The hard part is that it seems to last for such a long time.

We can adjust fairly quickly to other forms of loss—but not death. It cuts us deep and we wonder how long the intense sadness will last.

For a while.

DAY 292
SMARTIES

When asked if my cup is half-full or half-empty, my only response is that I am thankful that I have a cup.
—Sam Lefkowitz

IN AN ATTEMPT to offer a healthy snack, we gave our grandson Connor trail mix that included all types of nuts and a few *Smarties* mixed in.

We watched him separate the mix into two piles—a pile of nuts and a pile of sweet Smarties.

"You can have these, Grandpa," he said to me, pointing to the nuts. He chose the sweet things—the *Smarties*.

It reminded me that we need to find the sweet things in life—those precious moments even in the midst of our grief journey. This is true especially when there seem to be so many other things happening that are less palatable.

DAY 293
CLOCK

*When you arise in the morning, think of
what precious privilege it is to be alive—
to breathe, to think, to enjoy, to love.*
—Marcus Aurelius

The battery had run out. The clock had stopped. Time stopped.

That's what it feels like when someone dies—time stops. Why? Because we need it to.

Whether death was expected or sudden, we experience a period of shock following someone's death. We wish that we'd had more time with our loved one. Just another hug. One more conversation.

"I can't believe she's gone." And time grinds to a halt as we grieve.

Eventually the shock subsides, and we begin to realize that the minutes of our life still count. Recognizing that time is a precious commodity helps shape what we do next with it.

DAY 294
100%

A story should have a beginning, a middle and an end, but not necessarily in that order.
—Jean-Luc Godard

"I'M 100% BACK. I'm all good now."

Really? Are you sure?

Just a caution—grief will return and that "100%" may change.

I'm not trying to discourage you. I'm really not, but most people seem to have a collection of good and bad days in their transition through grief.

You might be feeling great today and find that tomorrow is a different story. Don't be disappointed or hard on yourself if grief comes back and you don't feel like you're a 10/10.

It's all part of adapting to a world that is new to you. Go with the flow. Be kind to yourself.

DAY 295
CURIOUS QUESTION #14

If you were to say one thing to your family about your loved one who died, what would it be?

EACH PERSON HAS a relationship with the one who died that is unique to them only. We all have a story with this person—it's filled with memories and experiences that are held as sacred.

As you grieve, it's important to share those unique stories with family members and friends. Then be sure to ask them what stories were most important to them.

When you have time to reflect during your grief journey, it's amazing how many stories come flooding back into your mind and heart.

DAY 296
YES

Two are better than one, because they have a good return for their labor. If either of them falls down, one can help the other up.
—Ecclesiastes 4:9-10

Is it a *yes* day? Perhaps you feel like it's a *no* day today: you don't feel like getting out, leaving the house or taking a phone call? If you've had a few of those in your week, it may be time for your own health's sake to say *yes* to today.

We all need community. We're built for it. Yes, there are times you need to be alone in your grief. Just be sure that you're not hiding.

Research indicates that spending too much time by ourselves can damage our emotional and physical health.

It might be important to say "yes" today and spend some time with people who care about you.

DAY 297
RESOLUTIONS

Hope is important because it can make the present moment less difficult to bear. If we believe that tomorrow will be better, we can bear a hardship today.
–Thich Nhat Hanh

A RESOLUTION IS A goal that you set and intend to make a habit. It may also be a dream that you've always had that you want to bring to fruition.

Do your dreams stop when someone dies? Some dreams can no longer be realized when a loved one dies. However, if you stop planning and dreaming, you stop believing and hoping for the future. "Without a vision, the people perish," goes the ancient proverb.

I wonder what resolutions you will put in place this year in order to accomplish your dreams.

We all need to believe in a future and a hope.

DAY 298
COIN

Our joys will be greater, our love will be deeper, our life will be fuller because we shared your moment.
—Unknown

I was surprised when I took out the $2 coin from my wallet. On one side, there was the usual head of Queen Elizabeth II, but on the other, was a sticker the size of the coin that simply said, "Thank You."

Think back to the moments you spent with your loved one who died. What do you think they would say about your relationship with them? What words would they use to express thanks to you?

Now think about those around you currently. What would you say to them to express your gratitude for their friendship or relationship with you?

"Thank You" carries a lot of weight in a grief journey.

DAY 299
SPARK

The past is a source of knowledge, and the future is a source of hope. Love of the past implies faith in the future.
—Stephen Ambrose

"It only takes a spark to get a fire going," say the lyrics of an old campfire song.

I love fires, especially on a cold evening. I especially love fires when shared with people who are special to me.

Are you missing someone?

Draw close to another person who is missing this person and warm up together.

DAY 300
BUFFERING

Wilderness is not a luxury but a necessity of the human spirit.
—Edward Abbey

IT DRIVES ME crazy when my computer is buffering—which happens frequently when I download a large amount of data and there are delays in transmission. I want it now—but I have to wait.

Buffering. That's a very apt metaphor for a grief journey. You're spinning, not going anywhere soon. Waiting. Wondering. It's a heavy transfer of information and emotion.

Some would call this place a *grief wilderness*, or a *dark night of the soul*. Regardless of the semantics it's a place where you feel stuck until you're ready to move forward into the unknown and discover a life that is different.

I'm wondering if *buffering* is something all of us need for a period of time.

DAY 301
PRINCIPLE

When we lose someone we love, we must learn not to live without them, but to live with the love they left behind.
—Unknown

Our values and principles help us navigate life. They are the compass that give us direction and help us make important decisions that will impact our next steps.

Are there any values or principles that you would like to carry forward that came from this person?

My grandma always reminded me to find the best in people. If I ever complained about a person or was negative, she'd stop me and remind me to find the good.

What value or principle have you taken into your life from the person who died—a value that's important to you?

DAY 302
OLIVES

*Sometimes you need to press pause
to let everything sink in.*
—Sebastian Vettel

Do you like olives? How about olive oil?
It takes a lot of olives to produce oil.
I don't like grief. I would rather not experience its pain. I feel pressed and squeezed at times and would prefer to run from its pressure.
Then I recognize what is slowly happening inside of me. Although it's difficult, it's producing some by-products in my life that are changing me in ways that are unexpectedly good.

DAY 303
SMELL

Smell is a potent wizard that transports you across thousands of miles and all the years you have lived.
—HELEN KELLER

HAVE YOU EVER been to your favourite restaurant and the smell of the food reminded you of the last time you were there with a certain person?

The sense of smell is closely linked to memory, probably more so than any of our other senses. It is also the sense that is most highly emotive. Smell plays a huge part in memory, mood and emotion. The perfumers and aromatherapy people totally get this.

Did your loved one have a special perfume or cologne that reminds you of them every time you open your closet? Where does that take you?

There can be so many smells that trigger memories. When they do, you need to prepare for grief to return but also for the memory and story to be honored.

DAY 304
LETTER

But grief is the ultimate unrequited love. However hard and long we love someone who has died, they can never love us back. At least that is how it feels.
—Rosamund Lupton, Sister

My son Landon reads it from time to time when he needs some loving words from his mom.

Before she died, Pam wrote a letter to each of her children to encourage them in their life journey following her death.

I'm not sure what Landon's letter says, but it's obviously meaningful since he holds onto it and keeps it close when he needs it.

You may not have a letter, but the words you remember coming from your loved on are significant.

Can you remember some of those words?

DAY 305
SURVIVOR

Where there is injury let me sow pardon.
—Francis of Assisi

When someone dies, we tend to view them in the best possible light after their death.

It's odd then that, as survivors, the opposite is true. We are often hard on ourselves saying, "I could have been or done more."

Survivor guilt frequently follows a loss.

Sometimes we get stuck in the past and believe that we were somehow "not enough." Truth be told, there is no perfect relationship. Things always could have been better. We wish we'd had more time with our loved one.

But what you did share was unique and meaningful—that's all that really matters. Let that be your focus: What you *did* have not what you *didn't*.

DAY 306
EARLY

Gratitude makes sense of our past, brings peace for today, and creates a vision for tomorrow.
—Melody Beattie

WE SPENT TIME with our family in the east today, celebrating Canadian Thanksgiving a week early.

Long distances can make it difficult to be together on a specific holiday. As I reflected upon that, I asked myself the question: "Why do we set aside one special day each year to give thanks when *every* day should be filled with gratitude?"

It also made me think about grief and how sometimes, in the midst of our deepest loss, we find it hard to be thankful because we are missing someone who was an integral part of our life.

Perhaps part of our grief journey is to find gratitude in midst of the sorrow and sadness.

What can I be thankful for today?

DAY 307
CAKE

*When someone you love becomes a memory,
that memory becomes a treasure.*
—Unknown

I USED TO PURCHASE an ice-cream cake every year for my first wife's birthday. I was never much of a baker, and she loved ice cream. So, it became a tradition.

Although Pam died years ago now, I still buy an ice cream cake on her birthday to honor her. My wife, Erica, listens to my stories about Pam as we reflect upon her legacy and enjoy the cake.

Connor, our eldest grandson, recently phoned and said, "Grandpa, guess what we're having tonight?" "What?" I asked. "An ice cream cake, because it's Grandma-in-heaven's birthday."

It's so important to remember and tell stories.

DAY 308
DOGS

Just play. Have fun. Enjoy the game.
—Michael Jordan

It wags its tail vigorously and looks up at me with big brown eyes. It bolts into the water and returns with the ball in its mouth, shakes the wet off its fur, soaking everything within a five-foot radius. Then it sees other puppies and hightails it to go play with them.

Dogs. They live to play.

We need to learn from them and play too, especially in the midst of our grief. Maybe you have a family pet. Or maybe you just need to *go out and play* with a friend. Hockey. Cribbage. Go to the zoo. Throw a frisbee around.

Just do it.

DAY 309
WEDDING

Those we love don't go away—they play beside us every day.
—U<small>NKNOWN</small>

W<small>E WENT TO</small> Saskatoon to celebrate the wedding of my nephew and his new bride. As I looked around, I thought about who was missing—my first wife, Pam, wasn't present. She had died a decade prior to this wonderful celebration.

When you gather family together for important life celebrations, you can't help but recognize who's *not* there—and wish they were. The *missing* intensifies.

It's amazing how the memory of a loved comes rushing back at family events when everyone's together.

I was sad, but amidst the celebrating realized something important: I miss because I still love—and that's a good thing.

DAY 310
ISLAND

To mourn your loss is required if you are to befriend the love you have been granted. To honor your grief is not self-destructive or harmful, it is life-sustaining and life-giving, and it ultimately leads you back to love again. In this way, love is both the cause and the antidote.

–Alan D. Wolfelt

"Yup! That would feel good about right now. Living on an island, where I can just be by myself—no one to bother me, talk to me or hug me. I've had enough of that for a while. I just want to be left alone."

Sound like you these days?

Are there times when you just need space? Then be honest with those around you. Let them know that this is temporary but necessary right now.

People worry about us when we spend too much time alone and wonder if we're turning inward.

We need *the island* at different times in our grief journey. It's okay.

Sail there when you need to but be sure to sail back to the *mainland* when you're ready.

DAY 311
BOOMERANG

You don't go around grieving all the time, but the grief is still there and always will be.
—Nigella Lawson

WHEN GRIEF RETURNS like a boomerang, it's better to tell people that you're experiencing a grief burst than to try and hide what's going on inside.

If a memory comes back, there's a reason it's returning, and you need to cherish it as a gift.

Our brains were created to store memories. Our senses trigger these memories whether taste, smell, touch, hearing or sight. Be certain that grief *will* come back, along with the memories of the life experiences that you shared together.

Memories are what connect us. So, let them come. And when they do, soak up all their goodness.

DAY 312
RESTORE

We build too many walls and not enough bridges.
—Isaac Newton

CHANGES IN RELATIONSHIPS are difficult to manage. We feel disappointed, sad and sometimes even angry. Consider the following questions as you sort out relationships that are still important to you but seem to have changed:

1. What relationship is different now that your loved one has died?
2. What is different about that relationship that concerns you?
3. Is the relationship important for you to continue? Why?
4. Is there something that you would like to say to this person that might help lighten your grief? Or lighten their grief?
5. Do you need to "let them off the hook" in order for that relationship to be restored?

DAY 313
HAT

Who am I to blow against the wind?
–Paul Simon

Have you ever noticed all the various types of hats that people wear?

Some hats protect us from the sun, others keep the rain from dowsing us, while others are a fashion statement, a sign of royalty or rank. Most hats are an identity statement of some type.

You may feel as though your identity is lost along with your loved one. You ask, "Who am I without this person in my life?" You are forced to wear a different hat, one that you didn't choose and that's not an easy fit: "I didn't want to be [single, alone, childless, etc.]." Fill in the blank. None of these were hats you had hoped for or planned.

But I always like to say this—you are made up of a whole bunch of different people who were a part of your life. So even if the person is no longer physically present anymore, they cannot be taken from you. They live on in you in some way.

DAY 314
SQUIRREL

The best way to pay for a lovely moment is to enjoy it.
—RICHARD BACH

SQUIRRELS GATHER NUTS prior to winter to help them make it through until the spring.

After loss it's a good idea to gather stories for the dark season of grief ahead, for the times when you know you'll miss your loved one and feel their absence.

Returning to these important stories will help you feel connected to the person you love and miss.

What special stories do you recall that bring that person closer to you?

DAY 315
ROUTINE

Some people don't like change, but you need to embrace change if the alternative is disaster.
–Elon Musk

It's Monday, the start of a new week. It's come way too fast.

Many people live for the weekends—if they are in jobs that permit them those days off. Weekends tend to bring people together.

Then comes Monday—people return to their homes or work, leaving you on your own. The support and social interaction you enjoyed for a couple of days are gone and you're left feeling lonely.

A big challenge in grief is accepting that people need to get back to their normal routine, even if you don't have your own as of yet. It's not easy to accept that when you feel disjointed following a loss.

Eventually you too will return to a routine. You'll look back and understand that this was all part of the grieving process.

DAY 316
CURIOUS QUESTION #15

Where has *Joy* taken you in the past?

WHEN YOU'RE SAD, it's hard to remember *Joy*. *Sad* is dark and lonely. It brings many tears. We need to cry in our grief journey, whether alone or with others.

It's okay say "hello" to *Sadness*, but it's also important to say "goodbye."

When we say "goodbye" to *Sadness*, it frees the pathway for *Joy* to return—it too was part of life in the past. Sometimes people feel that they don't deserve *Joy* in the midst of their grieving, but it's okay to want more *Joy*. Your loved one would want that for you.

When did you experience *Joy* in the past? Why not take time to write down some *Joy* moments and remind yourself how that felt? While recognizing that some of those *Joy* moments were with the person who has died, you've still experienced other *Joy* moments—they were just different.

Sometimes it's easy to forget the good things when we're swallowed up with *Sadness*. So, I encourage you to take some time to remember, allowing *Joy* to wash away some of the sorrow.

DAY 317
LENS

Knowing your purpose gives meaning to your life.
—Rick Warren

What do you see? Is grief clouding your vision for the future? It does that, doesn't it? But it also forces you to sit, ponder, miss, cry and eventually come to a place where you know that you'll be okay.

Not moving too quickly is really key for the griever. If you move too fast, you may find yourself making decisions that you'll regret or wish you had taken more time to discern.

This is not easy since you may feel stuck in your *new* life that has changed as a result of loss.

Viewing your life through a different lens will be helpful. One that says, "Slow down. Don't look too far ahead," will help uncloud your vision for the future. But in the meantime, focus on the *now* of what you are experiencing.

You will see a new day arrive in its time and the clouds will disappear.

DAY 318
SEASONS

If you're alive, there's a purpose for your life.
−Rick Warren

Depending on where you live, winter can be brutally cold. Those in frigid climates tend to hunker down and cuddle up in front of a fire with a warm blanket.

We all need warmth at times.

Grief can feel bitterly cold and then overwhelmingly hot at times.

Whatever temperature gauge you use to describe grief, know that the seasons of loss come and go. They are part of the grief journey.

Know that you will weather these "seasons"—and be okay.

DAY 319
MONEY

Life is full of grief, to exactly the degree we allow ourselves to love other people.
—Orson Scott Card, Shadow of the Giant

Has money become a problem in your family? It is for many families.

Money often creates undue stress and schisms for people following the death of a loved one.

Whether it be arguments over the estate or extra costs associated with funeral arrangements, money can be a separating factor for those who remain if you let it come between you.

It's sad if fighting over money is the biggest part of the days that follow the death of someone.

Is that really what your loved one would want for you and your family?

Consider the legacy of your family from your loved one's perspective and make your decisions based on their perspective: *What would Mom have wanted? What would Dad have wanted?*

DAY 320
TOSS

Trees love to toss and sway; they make such happy noises.
—EMILY CARR

IT WAS ONE of our favorite games as kids—the bean bag toss. It was a sloped board with one hole at the very top. Some versions have many holes and a point system, but this particular board only had one.

We'd take turns tossing the bean bags, challenging our hand-eye coordination. It was harder to sink that bean bag than you might think. We'd try tossing it different ways—each of us had our own technique that worked best for us.

Your grief journey is unique. You'll likely approach it from a different angle than someone else would.

Everyone's "toss" is different.

DAY 321
SENSITIVE

*Reckless words pierce like a sword, but the
tongue of the wise brings healing.*
—Proverbs 12:18

Remember to be sensitive to the person who is grieving differently from you. They had a different relationship with the one who died than you did.

Give each other grace in this journey. Communicate with those who are important to you. If they have distanced themselves from you, consider initiating the conversation by asking them how they think the relationship could best be restored and maintained.

This takes courage, but you will be empowered once you take that step. How about starting with:

"You are an important part of my life and I know that _____ was special to you also. I'm wondering if we can share in this grief journey together."

DAY 322
BREATH

*When you have lost hope, you have lost everything.
And when you think all is lost, when all is
dire and bleak, there is always hope.*
—Pittacus Lore

This week, our newborn grandbaby took his first breath.

This week, a dear friend of mine, who had struggled with cancer, took her last breath.

I sat back and marveled: One life begins and another ends.

One is just beginning his life; the other had a deep, long story-filled life with love and relationships.

But they had one thing in common—both were being held by people who loved them. Both had someone by their side, watching over them.

Having someone by your side when you are grieving gives you breath when you feel as though you are suffocating.

DAY 323
CORNER

*Still round the corner there may wait
a new road or a secret gate.*
–J. R. R. Tolkien

"It's just around the corner." Wouldn't that be great to hear? That the end of your grief journey could be in sight? People often ask, "How long will this grief last?" I wish that I could reassure them that the pain will be over once they round the bend.

The truth is, after loss, it's often grief that's just around the corner. Reminders are everywhere—things that you associate with your loved one. People feel badly for you and do their best to engage you, but they don't know what to say. You end up feeling all the more isolated.

In time, rounding the next corner won't include the intensity of the grief you feel right now, and you'll become less fearful about what's next.

DAY 324
GENTLENESS

We bereaved are not alone. We belong to the largest company in all the world—the company of those who have known suffering.
−Helen Keller

If there is one thing that we need from others during our grief journey, it's gentleness.

We are so fragile after a loss. It doesn't take much to break us.

Find people who are gentle in nature and invite them into your life.

You know who these people are.

DAY 325
REPEAT

Although it's difficult today to see beyond the sorrow, may looking back in memory help comfort you tomorrow.
—UNKNOWN

AND WHAT WILL you do when that person is not around for another family celebration or an important milestone event?

How will you manage your emotions when others are celebrating with their loved one and you're not?

Why not do some of the same things you did when you were together? Flowers, chocolates, dinner, games, cards, etc. Any way that you can connect and remember together with others is helpful when the celebration or event happens again this year.

Invite that person into your life for a moment.

DAY 326
SLIPPERY

Listen to what you know instead of what you fear.
—Richard Bach

BE CAREFUL NOT *to slip and fall. You might hurt yourself.* Depending upon where you live and the climate in your area, you know what footwear you need for the weather conditions. But sometimes, no matter how well-prepared you are, you still slip on the ice or wet pavement.

Making preparations is important in grief work. You do your best to weather grief, but some *grief seasons* are more difficult than others.

Grief is so unpredictable and changeable. Preparing for grief to return might help you prevent some big falls.

Where might you expect grief to return? How are you preparing for it?

DAY 327
COMMUNITY

The greatness of a community is most accurately measured by the compassionate actions of its members.
—Coretta Scott King

You are not alone. Remember that.

You need people in your life during your grief journey. Of course, you need time alone as well. But those who have an authentic and caring community are able to transition in their life and discover what's next much more easily than those who don't have a community to belong to. Research confirms this.

Isolation is hard on us. Don't try to go it alone when you are grieving.

Come out and find human connection with family and friends.

Reach out and find a community where you belong. Open up to someone who cares and will listen to your heart.

There are good people in the world who would be happy to come alongside you.

DAY 328
TIME

We must let go of the life we have planned, so as to accept the one that is waiting for us.
—Joseph Campbell

I WAS IN THE *right place at the right time.*
Grief however is never in the right place at the right time. It means the death of someone who was dear to you. There's never a good time for that.

I have heard some people say, "It was her time, so we have to accept it." "Our time will come soon enough," is often the next line. These are not un-truths, but they aren't helpful.

What *is* important is the time that you take to remember and integrate this person into your next chapter of life.

Don't pass over these minutes too quickly. Take some time to discover how this person will continue to be part of your life. Choose what you will bring along with you into your future.

DAY 329
QUESTIONS

He who would search for pearls must dive below.
—JOHN DRYDEN

"How come?" "What now?"

I hear these two questions so often after a person's loved one has died. But really, these two questions are two sides of the same coin. One looks back; one looks ahead.

Questions invite us to soul search. Dredging the depths of our experience, we are lured into finding meaning, rich as treasure, in the depths of our being. The answers are there.

Have you taken time to explore what's in your soul?

There you'll find truth that has always been but remained covert. By asking questions and reflecting deeply, you'll take notice of what wasn't previously seen. Especially in grief.

I wonder what you will find.

DAY 330
VALLEY

*The word happy would lose its meaning
if it were not balanced by sadness.*
—CARL JUNG

WHO LIKES TO suffer? Not me, and I believe not you either.

Grief brings suffering. I'm guessing you have asked this question in your grief: "I don't like the valley that I am in right now. How long will I be stuck in this place?"

But hold it…

Suffering won't defeat you. It hasn't in the past.

But it will meet you—it will meet you over and over again in life. Perhaps it's better to engage it while you're in the valley than to ignore it and let it grip you.

DAY 331
TELLING

Blessed are those who mourn, for they will be comforted.
—St. Matthew 5:4

It's a small world. Yesterday I met someone who knew my wife, Erica, from years ago. I learned some new things about Erica that I hadn't known before—details from her life as a young person that were new to me.

"Can you tell me a story?" That's one of the most powerful questions you can ask a person in their grief journey.

You long to remember the person who has died but become frustrated when people, with good but misguided intentions, tell you to "let go and move on." You can't just erase a relationship that was so important to you. There are so many things you miss.

Telling a story about your loved one is one of the best ways to move through grief in your way, at your pace. But it's important to ask others what they miss too—you just might hear some new stories that will bring joy to your heart.

DAY 332
DARK

*Hope is being able to see that there is
light despite all of the darkness.*
–Desmond Tutu

DARK IS DEFINED as the absence of light.
For the grieving heart, that's a space that feels grim, hopeless. Everything is darkness, you can't see your way clear to live fully again. You wonder if the pain of loss will ever subside.

Then there is this almost imperceptible sliver of light. When it enters your life, move toward it, hoping that there's more light where that came from.

And there is…

DAY 333
RITUAL

It's so curious: one can resist tears and 'behave' very well in the hardest hours of grief. But then someone makes you a friendly sign behind a window, or one notices that a flower that was in bud only yesterday has suddenly blossomed, or a letter slips from a drawer... and everything collapses.
—Colette

Ritual is a powerful tool. Especially when it's applied to your grief journey. Ritual allows you to find an enduring connection with your loved one who has died. Ritual is a way to keep their memory alive.

- What will you do to honor the person who died?
- What custom or practice will you repeat that will remind you of your loved one?
- Will you gather together for important events, holidays or anniversaries and intentionally remember this person?

What will your ritual of remembering look like, I wonder?

DAY 334
SLOW

We must accept finite disappointment, but never lose infinite hope.
—Martin Luther King, Jr.

I HAD A WART on the outside of my left pinkie toe, and it slowed me down—a lot!

Today, when I tried to charge through the mall to complete my chores, I couldn't because the wart was rubbing against the inside of my shoe. Such a small thing, but it hurt. It forced me to walk at a slower pace. To my surprise, I actually began to notice and enjoy everything around me. I really did.

Oh, how we need to live life differently and more intentionally.

It's the same with grief. Some people believe you should plough through it as fast as possible and get to the *other side* of it. I personally don't believe that's possible or healthy—grief has a purpose and requires that we slow down.

DAY 335
NEW

Ain't no shame in holding onto grief, as long as you make room for other things too.
—Bubbles, The Wire

WHY IS THAT others are uncomfortable with us just *staying put* after our loved one dies?

Sometimes we just need to say, "I don't want anything new in my life right now. I miss the old too much."

Isn't that fair?

Inside, we might be saying to ourselves: "I don't like being pushed. Please let me be the one to decide when it's time to change things up. Thanks for understanding where I'm at right now."

New is up to you.

DAY 336
SATELLITE

*If you want to understand today,
you have to search yesterday.*
—Pearl S. Buck

Where are you? Are you okay? I wish I could see your face and to hear your voice just one more time.

In loss, there is a desire for personal and physical connection again. We know the relationship will never be the same but we still long for what we had.

If you dig deep into your memory though, you will see and hear your loved one again.

What you hold dear is your shared story with this person. That's your satellite connection.

DAY 337
CURIOUS QUESTION #16

*What have you come to believe
about the soul and after life?*

When someone dies, often times people wonder where they have gone—or even if they have gone somewhere.

Where is my loved one?
Does their soul go somewhere?
Will I be able to see them again?
Do they see me?
Are they an angel?
How do I know they are okay?

Explore these deeper existential, spiritual questions by talking with others, reading about the afterlife or perhaps going on your own pilgrimage of understanding.

People in grief seem to need hope in order to move forward. Maybe this exploration could provide some meaning that you are desiring.

Ask yourself a question, "What do I need to learn that will give me peace?"

DAY 338
LAUGHTER

Smile—it improves your face value.
   –Ziggy

I love to belly laugh. We have all experienced a time when something strikes us as funny, and we can't stop laughing. It doesn't happen often, but the laughter is contagious when it does. Everyone around seems to *catch the laugh* as well.

I love being on a plane when a person watches a program on their iPad while wearing their headphones. Something they're watching makes them laugh out loud and they're completely unaware that others can hear them. I can't help but laugh with them, even if I don't know what they're laughing about.

The laughter is contagious.

Are you feeling particularly blue today? Maybe it's a good day to find a comedy to watch or enjoy a fun podcast.

Let yourself enjoy some laughter.

DAY 339
TRUTH

*There are moments in life when you miss someone
so much that you just want top pick them
from your dreams and hug them for real.*
—Charlie Brown

GRIEF IS AN opportunity to examine a relationship and perhaps discover that, while it wasn't perfect, it was still good.

Grief also has a way of changing our perception, causing us to idealize the one who has died. Then over time we realize that the relationship may have been a disappointment in some ways too. Surprising emotions can come to the fore as we face the truth about those disappointments.

Either way, we may feel guilty for being disappointed with the relationship or grieving something we never had.

The truth is they weren't perfect, but neither were you. Other parts of your loved one's life were good and really blessed you.

Focus on those things.

DAY 340
LEARNING

For as he thinketh in his heart, so is he.
–King Solomon

GRIEF IS A teacher. Does that sound strange to you? I wonder if loss isn't one of those life experiences that take us to deeper places of contemplation and reflection.

We don't choose grief, but it's here.

Perhaps honoring the grief and asking it some questions might also bring honor to the person who has died. They would want you to live in a joy-filled space.

What are you learning as you develop a relationship with Grief?

DAY 341
MOVE

Music is the soundtrack of your life.
–Dick Clark

I'VE ALWAYS ENJOYED music that had a good groove. It carries the piece forward. The movement of the rhythm and the steady beat make me want to join in—I want to sing, dance, move.

Grief has no rhythm. It is erratic, irregular, unpredictable.

Even if you wanted to move forward, grief can often stop you in your tracks…and bring the music to the halt. Or so it might seem.

What do you do when life has no rhythm? You shift the beat.

What can you do today to change the rhythm of your grief?

Why not dance and embrace the wonderful memory of the person who has died?

Take notice of what happens when you listen to the music "at a different tempo" and give it a place in your heart once more.

DAY 342
NOW

Just living is not enough—one must have sunshine, freedom, and a little flower.
—Hans Christian Andersen

We know that the sun will rise—even though it sets and disappears at night.

We expect spring to come—even on the heels of a cold winter.

Why? Because we have experienced these things repeatedly and know them to be true. We rest in the assurance that there will be a sunrise and a spring.

In grief, there are many unknowns. Perhaps you have had prior experience with a death or a loss. But not with this specific person, this unique relationship. Your future is unknown without them in your life.

In your grief journey, give thanks for what you had with this special person. Spend less time on what you didn't have. The future is unknown. But you have today—you always have today, every day. So, the question is: "What's good right now?"

DAY 343
PERSPECTIVE

*Grief is in two parts. The first is loss.
The second is the remaking of life.*
—Anne Roiphe

I ENJOY TRAVELING AND meeting new people because it gives me a different perspective on life.

All too easily, I get locked into my own thinking and miss out on new insights that I hadn't seen before.

Once my eyes are opened, I'm pleasantly surprised by what I learn. Had I stayed in one place, I never would have been able to see the world with different eyes. I would only have focussed on the difficult truth that my loved one was gone. I wouldn't be able to see my new identity.

How am I different now?

I wonder if a different perspective calls out to us as we struggle to transition into the next chapter of living?

DAY 344
PRESENCE

Grief and memory go together. After someone dies, that's what you're left with. And the memories are so slippery yet so rich.
—Mike Mills

GRIEF WILL RETURN—USUALLY unexpectedly. We also know that there are certain times of the year when we can expect it to resurface: holidays, birthdays, anniversaries, milestones and family celebrations.

These are memory-packed times that connect us to the past and can be enduring connections for the future.

If you plan ahead for these events, grief won't take you by surprise. Make an intentional plan to include your loved one in your family celebration.

There's an empty chair at the table during your celebration. How will you fill it with your loved one's presence?

DAY 345
LEAVES

Love is patient, love is kind. It does not envy, it does not boast, it is not proud. It does not dishonor others, it is not self-seeking, it is not easily angered, it keeps no record of wrongs.
—1 Corinthians 13:4-5

THEY CHANGED COLOR so quickly. Yesterday they were green. But when I went for a walk today, it seemed as though they had turned gold, red and orange overnight.

Sometimes relationships are like this as we begin our grief journey.

Following a loss, you may find that some of your relationships change quickly. People you thought would be there aren't. While others step up unexpectedly and are a tremendous support. Thank goodness for those people.

But for those who withdraw, there could be a myriad of reasons why they've chosen to do so. Instead of allowing your heart to be filled with anger, talk to the person and tell them what you miss about their relationship with you. The other option is to choose to spend time with people who support you.

Regardless—be proactive. You need people.

DAY 346
TOPPING

Miracles are retelling in small letters of the very same story which is written across the whole world in letters too large from some of us to see.
–C. S. Lewis

"What kind of topping do you want on your ice cream Sunday?" I ask the grandkids.

There were so many delicious and fattening options. My youngest grandson chose sprinkles and although that would not be my first pick, it was his. So, we ordered a bowl of vanilla ice cream bedecked with colorful sprinkles. Oh, and of course–a cherry on top.

If you were to think of one story about the person who died—one that is dear to you, describes them perfectly and that you'll never forget—what would that story be?

That might just be the "cherry on top" that you need to keep you going today.

DAY 347
23

Life after death is full of light and love.
—Sally Painter

It's not just another day of the year for me. I don't need to put it in my calendar because I will always remember it—the day my first wife died—July 23.

It was fifteen years ago today that Pam took her last breath at 6:20 a.m. It was a very sad day for me, for our family and close friends.

But for Pam it *was* just another number, because to her there was a "something next."

I find comfort in that.

DAY 348
FLOATERS

In any given moment we have two options: to step forward into growth or to step back into safety.
—Abraham Maslow

I have floaters in my eyes. There is nothing I can do about them I'm told. The optometrist said that my brain should adjust or perhaps the floaters will simply move to the periphery at some point. I don't like them at all—they bother me, especially in the bright sunlight. I wear my sunglasses, even in cloudy weather, so I don't have to see them. It helps—a little.

Grief is like that—it's something that gets in our way and clouds our vision. We hope that at some point it will move to the periphery.

It could be a death, or a family relationship that's difficult, a financial burden that needs time, or a hard feeling (like guilt) that just won't go away.

I wonder if you're able to change your focus and look to something that *does* bring you joy, something that doesn't cloud your vision.

DAY 349
GIVEN

The more you are grateful for what you have the more you will have to be grateful for.
−Zig Ziglar

LOOKING BACK. We all do that when someone special dies.

Sometimes we wish we had done things differently. Often, we wish we'd had more time.

Focussing our grief journey on what was given, not on what was taken, can be helpful even as we mourn.

We all wish for something different. But what is significant—always—is what was given.

And what was given is a good reason to give thanks.

DAY 350
GAME

You never know what you can do until you try, and very few try unless they have to.
−C. S. Lewis

I'M LEARNING TO enjoy board games—my children and grandchildren love them. For many years, I'd try to get out of playing them. *Surely there had to be more important things to do than sit for hours around a table with dice or cards?* It felt like a waste of time.

But how can spending time with people ever be a waste of time?

Even though you may not like a specific activity, there is value in hanging out with people during grief. You may even discover the activity you once disliked has now become one of your favorite things to do.

What activity will you choose to do—even though it may not have been part of your past experience?

DAY 351
TRANSITION

*All the art of living lies in a fine mingling
of letting go and holding on.*
–Havelock Ellis

The tension between old and new plays a dominant role in a person's grief journey.

Do you feel like a rubber band, stretched in opposite directions?

The invitation to enter a new life following the death of a loved one is perhaps one of the most difficult transitions you'll be forced to make. I say "forced," because you didn't ask for it.

It takes a lot of emotional effort to transition back into daily life without the presence of your loved one whom you miss.

Perhaps you can bring a little of that person with you into your next chapter.

DAY 352
WALKING

*Flowers are restful to look at. They have
neither emotions nor conflicts.*
—Sigmund Freud

I LOVE TO GO for walks with my wife, Erica.
It's a breakaway from life's busyness. It gets us out of our house and out of our heads and helps revive our souls.

Sometimes we walk and talk. Sometimes we're silent and just take in the fresh air and the fragrance of the poplar trees that are prolific in our area.

We need the space in our lives in order for silence to speak.

Go for a walk and breathe deeply.

DAY 353
BIRDS

A ship is safe in harbor, but that's not what ships are for.
—WILLIAM G.T. SHEDD

THEY'RE BACK.

Every morning at 5:30 a.m., I hear them singing. They are my alarm clock. They sing the same tune—joyful and familiar. The birds—wrens, jays, robins, woodpeckers and the Canada Geese, to name but a few—all singing in one enormously robust choir, right outside my window!

It's been a long time since they've woken me up in the morning, but now that it's spring, they greet the dawn with a (loud) song once again.

When experiencing loss, we wonder if joy will ever return to our lives. We wait. We wonder. We hope. We pray. It's winter. No spring in sight. Or so we think.

Then slowly, spring comes. We begin to hear a new song, one that we haven't heard for a while.

And we realize we are going to be okay after all.

DAY 354
FLIGHT

Don't be a leaf. Be a tree!
–Linus Van Pelt, Peanuts

HE LOOKED TO be about fifty years old. A farmer. As I sat down next to him, he immediately told me that this was his very first time on an airplane. I must confess I looked to see if there was a puke bag in the seat pocket in front of him—just in case. "So how are you feeling?" I asked him. "Good," he answered. "Excited!" he continued. I smiled. I hoped it would turn out well for him—and for me—and for the young girl in the window seat next to him whom he had also informed about *his maiden voyage*.

Grief really is an experience. It's all new. So different. And yet, we know that somehow, we are going to make it to the next destination. We need to.

When we started our descent, it got a little rough—he had a worried look on his face. Fortunately, it only lasted for a minute or two as the plane made its way through the clouds. Then we landed.

"So how was your first flight? Was it different from what you expected?" I asked. "Yes, it was, but it was good. I think I could do this again," he smiled.

DAY 355
TRAIN

When a train goes through a tunnel and it gets dark, you don't throw away the ticket and jump off. You sit still and trust the engineer.
—Corrie Ten Boom

I LEARNED SOMETHING INTERESTING about trains from living in the foothills of the Rocky Mountains: It takes two engines to get a train through a steep mountain pass.

I used to read that famous children's book to my kids, *The Little Engine That Could*. I always admired the gumption of that little train going it alone and making it up and over the other side.

Wouldn't it be nice if there were actually two engines to pull you over your deepest mountains of grief? But there aren't—you're only one person. I'm not saying to go it alone though—other people can be tremendous supports in your grief journey. They can help you move forward.

But ultimately, you're one person on a personal grief journey. No one else can live your experience.

Here's the truth though—you have the gumption you need to make it. Believing in your ability to be resilient is something worth believing in.

You think you can? You knew you could! You knew you could!

DAY 356
SPRING

Hope is the thing with feathers that perches in the soul and sings the tune without the words and never stops at all.
—Emily Dickinson

SIGNS OF SPRING. Delicate blossoms. Green buds like lace on the trees. Bird songs early in the morning. Life that was hidden during the winter is finally pushing through. We are in a new and different season.

You have the heard phrase, "Seeing is believing." In grief, much of what is happening you can't see. You feel as though you are still living in winter—it's cold and bleak. You are waiting for spring to arrive in your life.

In grief, there is always winter. The only way for spring to appear is to encounter winter first. But take courage…

Spring is coming. It always does.

DAY 357
GATHERING

Make today worth remembering.
–Zig Ziglar

We will be gathering together as a family—but someone will be missing.

It's hard. We miss her so much.

But we still get together, because we are still a family.

Our oldest grandson, Connor, and his dad are "gathering" today. It's a different type of gathering—it's called bailing. The crops are ready, and they will gather the hay into bails and store it for future use. They don't need it right now, but someday they will.

They are planning ahead.

Family gatherings are important. They require planning—especially when someone is missing who used to be a big part of precious celebrations.

At your next family gathering, give that person whom you miss a place in your day.

Tell a story, light a candle, continue a tradition, create a new one, make their favorite food.

Whatever you do, do it together. And remember.

DAY 358
CURIOUS QUESTION #17

**What is becoming clear to you as
you think about your future?**

CLARITY IN THE midst of grief is something worth celebrating. There are so many decisions that impact your future.

Grief presents you with possibilities. Having the clarity to discover what's next is a gift to yourself and those around you.

You've had time to reflect upon your future. Perhaps it's time to take some small steps forward. Small steps—not huge leaps. That's important.

What steps have you already taken that have been helpful for you? What steps do you plan on taking that will give you confidence and the assurance that you'll be okay?

DAY 359
GARDEN

Mondays aren't that bad. They help us appreciate the rest of the days of the week.
—Ziggy

We dug rows in the dirt and sowed the seeds, covered them over with black earth and waited for them to grow.

While we couldn't see what was happening beneath the soil, we believed and hoped that something would spring to life. We'd check daily to see if there were signs of new life in our little garden.

It took a while, but one day, out of the darkness, green shoots emerged—tiny garden miracles.

In the darkness of grief, we wonder if anything good could ever grow in us again. The garden of our hearts lie fallow—or so we think.

But slowly, over time, tiny miracles of life begin to resurface. And we realize that we are going to be okay after all.

We just needed to be patient.

DAY 360
DOOR

*When the heart grieves over what it has lost,
the spirit rejoices over what it has left.*
—SUFI PROVERB

"WHAT'S BEHIND DOOR number two?" is a familiar question on the *Let's Make a Deal* game show.

Being willing to take a chance and open up the next door isn't always easy after the loss of a loved one.

We prefer to play it safe and not choose any door, but life calls us to what's next. That's transition—and it's scary.

Opening up that door can lead to love and joy.

I wonder if your loved one who has died isn't at that door, helping you walk through it. You'll never know until you turn the handle.

DAY 361
PEN

Grief can be the garden of compassion. If you keep your heart open through everything, your pain can become your greatest ally in your life's search for love and wisdom.

—Rumi

How do you write the next part of your story when the person who has died is no longer part of it? I'm not sure, but maybe you need to ask them.

They knew you well. What would they say to you? What would their hopes and dreams be for you? Include them in your next chapter. They know you.

Perhaps they might help you *co-author* your next chapter of life. Listen carefully to what they would say to you.

DAY 362
BLOOM

Grief does not change you, Hazel. It reveals you.
–John Green

Depending upon where you live, the flowers begin blooming at different months of the year.

I love it when flowers begin to bloom, and buds appear on trees signaling that the cold winter is over. The weather is warming, allowing new growth to emerge.

Spring can come so quickly that it surprises you.

I think this happens in the grief journey as well.

If grief is like being in the dead of winter, then spring is like emerging to look at life with fresh eyes and a renewed sense of hope.

We all bloom again.

DAY 363
RARE

Perhaps they are not stars in the sky, but rather openings where our loved ones shine down to let us know they are happy.
—Inuit proverb

I used to collect hockey cards when I was young. I had the Bobby Orr rookie card. And many more precious cards that are valuable. They have become rare.

What makes something rare?

It seems that it has to be something that's old or an item that's a limited edition, like a Van Gogh painting or a baseball signed by Babe Ruth.

Your loved one was one of a kind. You have painted a picture of them in your mind, created a portrait that will remain forever.

Others who knew this person, will have a different picture of them. But to you, this who they were and always will be.

DAY 364
365

*The good life is a process, not a state of being.
It is a direction not a destination*
—Carl Rogers

There's nothing magical about the number 365 in grief—not unless you want there to be.

Why? Because grief doesn't run on a daily, monthly or yearly schedule.

Yes, "firsts" without your loved one are significant—first Christmas, first birthday, first grandchild, first anniversary—but if you do those *firsts* well, embracing the memory of your loved one, you will look differently upon your grief.

Grief will always be at your door, because you will always miss. Some days will be lighter than others, but 365 is just a number.

Don't let it be anything more than that in your grief journey.

DAY 365
THERMALS

We keep moving forward, opening new doors, and doing new things, because we're curious and curiosity keeps leading us down new paths.
—Walt Disney

Yesterday, my wife and I saw two eagles soar across the background of the azure blue sky. What we noticed was that they never flapped their wings. All they did was adjust to the thermals and catch the next lift. Then they soared. It was inspiring to watch.

Thermals are columns of air created by uneven heating on the earth's surface. The very thing that creates instability is the thing that gives the eagle its flight.

Life wants to give us something if we are willing to discover what it might be. The key is being willing to adjust to the thermals—and soar.

For over thirty-nine years Rick Bergh has been involved in various aspects of death, dying and grief as a thanatologist, his wealth of experience resulting in nine published books on the subject.

Trained in narrative therapy, Rick's grief and loss practice has provided him with valuable information from people who have "lived grief experience" and have come out the other side to encounter joy once more.

In his popular grief podcast, *It's All About the Story*, Rick interviews everyday people about their grief stories. These individuals openly provide valuable insights from their lived experience—wisdom not often found in textbooks.

Rick's career as counsellor, podcaster, online educator, workshop leader, pastor, chaplain, speaker, writer and researcher has allowed him to share his message with a variety of audiences.

> *Grief Start*™, the practical online grief course developed by Rick, allows people to work through their grief journey in the convenience of their own home, in their own time. The modules include videos and downloadable PDFs to support those who are going through a grief journey themselves

or those who want to learn how to help others who are grieving.

All Things Grief will offer you access to Rick's resource library including lectures, workshop, webinars, blogs, online grief courses, papers, research and so much more. With one click you can bypass the *World Wide Web* and access the entirety of trusted information about grief and loss found on Rick's platform.

For more information about any of the above, please visit **www.rickbergh.com**

www.ingramcontent.com/pod-product-compliance
Lightning Source LLC
Chambersburg PA
CBHW021146060526
44107CB00146B/1331/J